Student Study Guide
to accompany

Management
A Real World Approach

First Edition

Andrew Ghillyer, Ph.D.
Vice President of Academic Affairs
Argosy University, Tampa, Florida

Prepared by
Amit Shah
Frostburg University

 **McGraw-Hill**
Higher Education

Boston   Burr Ridge, IL   Dubuque, IA   New York   San Francisco   St. Louis
Bangkok   Bogotá   Caracas   Kuala Lumpur   Lisbon   London   Madrid   Mexico City
Milan   Montreal   New Delhi   Santiago   Seoul   Singapore   Sydney   Taipei   Toronto

The **McGraw·Hill** Companies

 **McGraw-Hill Higher Education**

Student Study Guide to accompany
MANAGEMENT: A REAL WORLD APPROACH
ANDREW GHILLYER

Published by McGraw-Hill Higher Education, an imprint of The McGraw-Hill Companies, Inc., 1221 Avenue of the Americas, New York, NY 10020.

2 3 4 5 6 7 8 9 0 QSR/QSR 11 10

ISBN: 978-0-07-7230401
MHID: 0-07-723040X

www.mhhe.com

Chapter 1: What Is Management?

LEARNING GOALS

After you have read this chapter, you should be able to:

1. Define Management.
2. Identify and explain the levels of management.
3. Explain the management process.
4. Explain the basic principles of management.
5. Identify the changing nature of the manager's environment.

LEARNING THE LANGUAGE

Listed below are important terms found in the chapter. Choose the correct term for each definition and write it in the space provided.

Business Ethics	Middle Management
Organizing	Controlling
Diversity	Senior Management
Glass Ceiling	Supervisory Management
Planning	Staffing
Conceptual Skills	Role
Human Relations Skills	Technical Skills
Management	Leading

1. The process of deciding the best way to use an organization's resources to produce goods or provide services is called Management

2. Diversity in the workforce means including people of different genders, races, religions, nationalities, ethnic groups, age groups, and physical abilities.

3. The front-line level of management is Supervisory Management and these employees make sure that the day-to-day operations of the organization run smoothly.

4. _Glass ceiling_ is an invisible barrier that prevents women and minorities from moving up in the organizational hierarchy.

5. _Conceptual Skills_ involve understanding the relationship of the parts of a business to one another and to the business as a whole.

6. _Human Resource Skills_ _____ are those that managers need to understand and work well with people.

7. Employees who are responsible for meeting the goals that senior management sets are referred to as _Middle Management_.

8. The specific abilities that people use to perform their jobs are referred to as _Technical Skills_

9. A(n) _Role_ is a set of behaviors associated with a particular job.

10. _Business Ethics_ involves the application of standards of moral behavior to business situations.

11. _Senior Management_ _____ is the highest level of management and establishes the goals or objectives of the organization.

12. Determining human resource needs and recruiting, selecting, training, and developing human resources refers to _Staffing_

13. _Controlling_ refers to measuring performance against objectives, determining the causes of deviations, and taking corrective action where necessary.

14. The process of deciding what objectives to pursue during a future time period and what to do to achieve those objectives is called _planning_

15. _Leading_ refers to directing and channeling human behavior toward the accomplishment of objectives.

16. Grouping activities, assigning activities, and providing the authority necessary to carry out the activities is called _organizing_

ASSESSMENT CHECK

Learning Goal 1
Define Management.

1. What are some of the things a manager must do?

   Plans how to utilize the Overall resourses of the Company.

2. An organization's resources include:

   Employees, Equipments, and money.

Learning Goal 2
Identify and Explain the Levels of Management.

3. What is the highest level of management and what are its important functions? *Senior Management*

   Establishes the goals, or objectives, of the organization.

4. What are the responsibilities of middle management?

   Meeting the goals that senior management sets.

5. What is another name for front-line management? Who do they oversee? *Supervisory Management.*

   They make sure that the day-to-day operations of the organization run smoothly.

6. What do the three levels of management form? Define this term.

   Hierarchy, or a group ranked in order of importance

Learning Goal 3
Explain the Management Process.

7. What are three ways to examine how management works?

    Senior Management

    Middle Management

    Supervisory Management

8. What are the five categories of management tasks?

    1. Planning
    2. organizing
    3. staffing
    4. Leading
    5. Controlling

9. Henry Mintzberg's research identified key managerial roles, which are split into three categories. Identify the roles in each category.

Interpersonal: the figurehead

Informational: the disseminator

Decisional: the entrepreneur

10. Briefly describe the three types of skills required to perform a particular job. *Conceptual skills: understanding how different parts of companies relate.*
Human Relations skills: Needed to work well with other Companies.
Technical skills: used to perform jobs.

Learning Goal 4
Explain the basic principles of management.

11. What agreement must you abide by in order to pursue the fulfilling and rewarding job of a manager? *Expected to set the standard for your department and model the behavior you expect from your people.*

Learning Goal 5
Identify the changing nature of the manager's environment.

12. What are two factors that can improve the quality of work life for employees?

13. Despite positive changes that have occurred over the last several decades, most senior managers in the U.S. are still white men, perpetuating what specific problem?

CRITICAL THINKING EXERCISES

Learning Goals 1 and 2

1.   Consider your college or university or, if you are employed, consider the company for which you work:

a.   Who are your senior managers, middle managers, and supervisory managers? 1. chair person, chief executive, chief operating, senior vice p. 2. Department head, sales manager 3. Foreman, crew leader, store manager.

b.   How is the organizational hierarchy shaped? A pyramid.

c.   What changes would you make to improve the operations?

Learning Goal 3

2.   Think of your student life in this class. How would you apply the three management skills to your student life in this management class? Each one would be applied to my every day life in the job force in order to find success.

Learning Goal 4

3.   Consider the company for which you work. If you are promoted to a
     managerial position, how will your job change? Consider factors such
     as job responsibilities, employee interaction, and your philosophies
     about work. I will have to maintain a staff that completes their
     job assignment. This will help to generate commitment
     throughout the job force.

Learning Goal 5

4.   Think of a company with which you are familiar. How diverse is the
     organization? Does the diversity of the company play a role in their
     competitiveness? Would you like to work for this company? Why or
     why not? Walmart is very diverse. Being that people of different
     back grounds and customs shop there all of the time, the
     company has an edge over competition.

PRACTICE TEST

MULTIPLE CHOICE – Circle the best answer.

Learning Goal 1
1. What is the process of deciding the best way to use an organization's resources to produce goods and services?
   a. Leadership
   b. Resource allocation
   c. Management
   d. Planning

2. An organization's resources include all of the following except:
   a. Employees
   b. Competitors
   c. Equipment
   d. Money

Learning Goal 2
3. What level of management is responsible for meeting goals that senior management sets?
   a. Senior management
   b. Middle management
   c. Supervisory management
   d. Employee management

4. Which of these levels of management is the highest level?
   a. Senior management
   b. Middle management
   c. Supervisory management
   d. Employee management

5. The three levels of management form _____.
   a. organizational skills
   b. managerial functions
   c. organizational creativity
   d. a hierarchy

Learning Goal 3

6.   What is the set of behaviors associated with a particular job?
        a.   A role
        b.   A management level
        c.   A skill
        d.   An employee

7.   Which category of management tasks describes when a manager groups related activities together and assigns employees to perform them?
        a.   Controlling
        b.   Organizing
        c.   Leading
        d.   Planning

8.   Which category of management tasks describes when a manager provides the guidance employees need to perform their tasks?
        a.   Controlling
        b.   Organizing
        c.   Leading
        d.   Planning

9.   When a manager performs symbolic duties as head of the organization, this is referred to as a _____.
        a.   spokesperson
        b.   figurehead
        c.   leader
        d.   liaison

Learning Goal 4

10.   Which of the following phrases best describes the management agreement?
        a.   "With responsibility comes a larger salary."
        b.   "With power comes more prestige."
        c.   "With power comes responsibility."
        d.   "With responsibility comes more employees."

11.   The rapid change in information availability _____ technological change.
     a.   only slightly decreases
     b.   decreases
     c.   has no effect on
     (d.)   increases

12.   The latest demographic information shows that the United States is becoming _____.
     (a.)   older and more diverse
     b.   younger and less diverse
     c.   younger and more diverse
     d.   older and less diverse

TRUE-FALSE

Learning Goal 1
1.   Employees are not considered an organizational resource. F

Learning Goal 2
2.   Supervisory management is responsible for meeting the goals that senior management sets. F

3.   Middle management sets goals for specific areas of the organization and decides what the employees in each area must do to meet those goals.

Learning Goal 3
4.   Planning occurs when a manager decides on a set of goals and the actions the organization must take to meet them. T

5.   A manager is conducting an act of controlling when they measure how the organization performs to ensure that financial goals are being met. T

6.   A leader role is where the manager develops and maintains the different webs of contact outside the organization.

7. The disseminator role is where the manager gives other people the information they need to make decisions. *T*

8. Conceptual skills are most vital for supervisory managers. *F*

9. Human relation skills are those that managers need to understand and work well with people. *T*

Learning Goal 4

10. As a manager you will be expected to set the standard for your department and to model the behavior you expect from your people. Therefore, you will no longer be able to put yourself before others. *F*

Learning Goal 5

11. The United States is becoming older and less diverse, according to the latest demographic information.

12. "Doing the right thing" describes business propensity.

ANSWERS

LEARNING THE LANGUAGE

1. Management	9. Role
2. Diversity	10. Business Ethics
3. Supervisory Management	11. Senior Management
4. Glass Ceiling	12. Staffing
5. Conceptual Skills	13. Controlling
6. Human Relations Skills	14. Planning
7. Middle Management	15. Leading
8. Technical Skills	16. Organizing

ASSESSMENT CHECK

1. Managers must make good decisions, communicate well with people, make work assignments, delegate, plan, train and motivate people, and appraise employees' job performances.

11

2. An organization's resources include its employees, equipment, and money.

3. The highest level of management is senior management and they are responsible for establishing the goals or objectives of the organization. They decide which actions are necessary to meet those goals and how to use the organization's resources.

4. Middle management is neither highest nor lowest in an organization and must report to senior management.

5. Another name for the front-line level of management is supervisory management. They oversee the operatives.

6. The three levels of management form a hierarchy, or a group ranked in order of importance.

7. The three ways to examine how management works includes a) dividing the tasks that managers perform into categories, b) looking at the roles that different type of managers play in a company, and c) looking at the skills that managers need to do their jobs.

8. The five categories of management tasks are planning, organizing, staffing, leading, and controlling.

9. The 10 key managerial roles are split into interpersonal: figurehead, leader and liaison; informational: monitor, disseminator, and spokesperson; and decisional: entrepreneur, resource allocator and negotiator.

10. Three types of skills are:
(1) Conceptual skills – those that help managers understand how different parts of a company relate to one another and to the company as a whole;
(2) Human relations skills – those that managers need to understand and work well with people; and
(3) Technical skills – the specific abilities that people use to perform their jobs.

11. The management agreement must be abided by in order to pursue the fulfilling and rewarding job of a manager.

12. The quality of work life for employees can be improved by 1) safe and healthy working conditions, 2) opportunities to use and develop initial capabilities, 3) opportunity for personal and professional growth, 4) work schedules, career demands, and travel requirements that do not regularly take up family and leisure time, and 5) the right to personal privacy, free speech, equitable treatment, and due process.

13. The problem of the glass ceiling – the invisible barrier that prevents women and minorities from moving up in the organizational hierarchy – still remains.

CRITICAL THINKING EXERCISES

1. a. Student answers may vary. It is important for students to recognize the differences between management and their roles in the organization.

    b. An organizational hierarchy will be shaped like a pyramid.

    c. Student responses will vary.

2. This is an interesting exercise to understand that management skills are also applicable to just about everything you manage or engage in. As a student in this management class, you will have to plan your work, semester/quarter, and how you are going to meet the requirements of the class, as well as what grade you want and how you will go about achieving it. These activities are part of planning function and require conceptual skills. The human relations skills will come into play, as you need to interact with your professor and other students in team/class. Finally, the actual task of studying, learning, and performing in the class requires technical skills.

3. Being promoted to a managerial position will alter the way you previously viewed your work. The biggest difference is the level of responsibility you will have when you receive a promotion. You will no longer be able to hang out as much with your operatives/subordinates, play favorites, put yourself ahead of others,

pass the buck on difficult assignments, or bring your personal problems to work.

4. Student answers may vary. It is important to point out that diversity can give an organization a competitive advantage. For example, if all of the employees think and act the same, creativity will not exist. Companies that are able to produce innovative products will have an advantage over other companies in any industry.

PRACTICE TEST

MULTIPLE CHOICE

1. C	7. B
2. B	8. C
3. B	9. B
4. A	10. C
5. D	11. D
6. A	12. A

TRUE FALSE

1. False	7. True
2. False	8. False
3. True	9. True
4. True	10. True
5. True	11. False
6. False	12. False

Chapter 2- A Brief History of Management

After you have read this chapter, you should be able to:

1.   Explain the role of the Industrial Revolution in the development of managerial thought and identify the captains of Industry and their role in management's evolution.
2.   Define scientific management and outline the role of Frederick W. Taylor played in its development.
3.   Identify and explain the human relations movement.
4.   Explain the systems approach.
5.   Explain the differences between Theory X, Theory Y, and Theory Z.
6.   Define the contingency approach to management.
7.   Explain the concepts of the search for excellence and the emphasis on quality.
8.   Understand what is required for an organization to move from good to great.

LEARNING THE LANGUAGE

Listed below are important terms found in the chapter. Choose the correct term for each definition and write it in the space provided.

Closed system	Scientific management
Contingency approach to management	Soldiering
Functions of management	System
Hawthorne effect	Theory X
Hedgehog concept	Theory Y
Industrial revolution	Theory Z
Motion study	Professional manager
Open system	

1. Hawthorne Effect ~~The~~ states that giving special attention to a group of employees changes their behavior.

2. In order to find the 'one best way' to perform a task, Frederick W. Taylor, began to measure individual tasks within jobs, measuring both the time taken to do the task and observing the motions involved. This was referred to as Time and Motion Study

3. Theory Y _____ managers believe employees can be trusted to meet production targets without being threatened and, therefore, manage in a democratic and participative manner.

4. A(n) Closed System does not interact with their external environments.

5. The Hedgehog Concept was drawn from Isaiah Berlin and suggests that great companies develop a simple core concept that guides all their future strategies, as opposed to chasing every new management fad or policy implementation.

6. The Industrial Revolution started in 1860 and encompassed the period when the United States began to shift from an almost totally farming-based society to an industrialized society.

7. Soldiering describes the actions of employees who intentionally restrict output.

8. A(n) Open System is influenced by its internal and external environmental factors and creates a dynamic relationship.

9. Theory Z _____ was developed by William Ouchi and attempts to integrate American and Japanese management practices by combining the American emphasis on individual responsibility with the Japanese emphasis on collective decision making, slow evaluation and promotion, and holistic concern for employees.

10. The philosophy of Frederick W. Taylor that seeks to increase productivity and make the work easier by scientifically studying work methods and establishing standards is called Scientific Management

11. The *Contingency Approach to Management* _____ theorizes that different situations and conditions require different management approaches.

12. A(n) *system* is "an assemblage or combination of things or parts forming a complex or unitary whole."

13. *Theory X* _____ managers manage in a very controlling and authoritative manner.

14. The *Function of Management* _____ consist of planning, organizing, commanding, coordinating, and controlling.

15. A(n) *Professional Manager* _____ is a career person who does not necessarily have a controlling interest in the company for which he or she works.

ASSESSMENT CHECK

Learning Goal 1
Explain the role of the Industrial Revolution in the development of managerial thought and identify the captains of Industry and their role in management's evolution.

1. What were the three components used to describe the Industrial Revolution by Daniel Wren? Briefly explain each component.
   Power: New inventions, such as the steam engine, allowed industries to expand. Transportation: Moved through periods of industrial and commercial traffic communication. By way of telegraph, telephone, and radio changed the way U.S. organizations functioned.

2. What industries were the four captains famous for?
   Oil, Tobacco, steel, steamships/Railroad

3. What legislative act was passed to regulate business and check corporate practices? *The Human Resource movement*

Learning Goal 2

Define scientific management and outline the role of Frederick W. Taylor played in its development.

4.　　What was the reason Taylor found that explained why employees were "soldiering"?

Employees were intentionally restricting output.

5.　　List the four main principles of scientific management.

The development of a scientific method of designating jobs to replace the old rule-of-thumb method.

The scientific selection and progressive teaching and development of employees.

The bring together of scientifically selected employees and scientifically developed methods for designing jobs.

A division of work resulting in interdependence between management and workers

6.　　What was the philosophy behind Taylor's scientific management?

~~old rule of thumb method~~

7.　　Who was Henry Lawrence Gantt and what was he famous for?

A colleague of Taylor who helped to promote scientific management.

famous for production control.

Learning Goal 3
Identify and explain the human relations movement.

8.　　What research project ignited the interest of business in the human element of the workplace? Briefly describe the project.

The Hawthorne studies.

It defines the relationship between physical working condition and worker productivity.

9.　　Who was Chester Barnard and how did he view organizations?

president of New Jersey Bell Telephone.

He viewed organization as a social ~~structures~~ structure

Learning Goal 4
Explain the systems approach.

10. Name and describe the two types of systems? Open system: interacts with its external environment.

closed system: Has no interaction with its external environment

Learning Goal 5
Explain the differences between Theory X, Theory Y, and Theory Z.

11. Douglas McGregor proposed a simple division of management styles. What were the two management styles and how did they differ?

~~Theory X & Theory Y.~~ Theory X: Controlling/authoritative Managers
Theory Y: Democratic/Participative Managers

12. How was Theory Z developed and what does it attempt?

In acknowledgment to Douglas McGregor's Theory X and Theory Y.
It attempts to integrate American and Japanese management practices,

Learning Goal 6
Define the contingency approach to management.

13. What does the contingency approach to management theorize and in which areas has this theory been further developed/used?

outline in detail the style or approach that works best under certain circumstances.

used in decision making, organizational design, leadership, planning, and group behavior.

Learning Goal 7
Explain the concepts of the search for excellence and the emphasis on quality.

14. What are Peters and Waterman's eight characteristics of excellent companies? Briefly describe each.

1. A Basis For action 2. close to the customer 3. Autonomy and Entrepreneurship

4. Productivity through people 5. Hands on: Value driven 6. stick to the knitting

7. simple form: lean staff, 8. Simultaneous Loose-tight properties

15. What change took place starting in the late 1970s and why did this change take place?

Peters & Waters used a combination of their own standards & six measures of financial success covering a 20-year period studied.

Reemphasized the value of on-the-job experimentation and creative thinking

Learning Goal 8

Understand what is required for an organization to move from good to great.

6. What is the hedgehog concept?

Focussing on simple, basic principles that allow the company to focus on performance rather than pursuing several strategic projects at the same time.

CRITICAL THINKING EXERCISES

Learning Goal 1

1. The Industrial Revolution began in 1860, almost 150 years ago. Have we had any revolutions since then? What are some possible changes that may occur in the future that would bring about another revolution?

Learning Goal 2

2. Many organizations today have been organized around principles developed by Henri Fayol. Read the following and determine if these are his ideas being described. Write "Yes" if it's a Fayol idea; "No" if it's not.

a. ___Y___ Introduced several "principles" of organizing.

b. ___Y___ Believed workers should think of themselves as coordinated teams, and that the goal of the team is more important than individual goals.

c. ___N___ Promoted a bureaucratic organization.

d. ___N___ Believed that large organizations demanded clearly established rules and guidelines, which were to be precisely followed.

e. ___Y___ Wrote that each worker should report to only one boss.

f. ___Y___ Said that managers should treat employees and peers with respect.

g. ___Y___ Wrote that functions are to be divided into areas of specialization such as production, marketing and so on.

h. ___N___ Believed in written rules, decision guidelines and detailed records.

i. ___N___ Said that staffing and promotions should be based solely on qualifications.

j. ___N___ Proposed that an organization should consist of three layers of authority: top managers, middle managers, and supervisors.

k. ___N___ Believed the less decision making employees had to do, the better.

1._____Y_____ Believed that managers have the right to give orders and expect obedience.

Learning Goal 3

3. Think of a time when you were at work and you had a task to perform with no supervision. Think of a time when a group of you and your co-workers worked together with your manager to meet a deadline.

    a. Did you work harder when you were by yourself or with your manager? Why?
    b. What effect is being portrayed in this example?

Learning Goal 5

4. Describe a past or current manager that you have experienced. Classify him/her as a Theory X or Theory Y manager and provide examples that support your assessment.

Learning Goal 6

5. John is a manager at a grocery store. Greg and Tom are two of his employees. John must manage each of these two differently. Greg is an unmotivated employee who needs to be pushed to complete his duties. Tom, on the other hand, can be given a task and could complete it with no further oversight. Describe what is taking place in this scenario and style of management John should utilize.

Learning Goal 7

6. Company A and company B are both very successful. Company A developed a few products that have been really popular and has not had to develop any other new products. Company A has been following a strict set of rules that has led to their success. Company B has had to adapt to consumer preferences, constantly introducing new products and changing the rules of the organization. Which company will remain successful longer and why?

Learning Goal 8

7. McDonald's, famous for its burgers, also owned Donato's Pizzeria, Boston Market, and Chipotle. McDonald's sold both Donato's and Boston Market, and has significantly reduced its ownership shares in Chipotle. Why do you believe McDonald's might make such a move? What concept does this move illustrate? Explain.

PRACTICE TEST

MULTIPLE CHOICE – Circle the best answer.

Learning Goal 1

1. Which of the following is not one of the three components that described the Industrial Revolution in America?
   a. Power
   b. Communication
   c. Money
   d. Transportation

2. Who of the following is not considered one of the captains of industry?
   a. John D. Rockefeller
   b. Cornelius Vanderbilt
   c. Andrew Carnegie
   d. Frederick Taylor

Learning Goal 2

3.   Frederick W. Taylor developed what philosophy?
      a.   Piece-rate systems
      (b.)   Scientific management
      c.   Functions of management
      d.   Hawthorne effect

4.   Scientific management is a philosophy about:
      (a.)   the relationship between people and work.
      b.   businesses in the chemical industry.
      c.   a technique used to increase quality.
      d.   an efficiency device.

5.   What was Henri Fayol's greatest contribution?
      a.   Piece-rate systems
      b.   Scientific management theory
      c.   Gantt chart
      (d.)   Principles of management

Learning Goal 3

6.   What does the Hawthorne effect state?
      a.   Constant supervision is needed for employees to stay on task.
      b.   Laissez-faire style management increases production and employee morale.
      (c.)   Giving special attention to a group of employees changes their behavior.
      d.   Employees are more productive when left alone to perform tasks.

7.   What did researchers first do in the Hawthorne studies to test productivity?
      (a.)   Lowered the level of lighting.
      b.   Increased wages.
      c.   Changed the length of the workday.
      d.   Increased rest periods.

8.   It was after the _____, during the period known as
      _____ that legislatures and courts actively supported organized
      labor and the worker.
      a.   Golden Age of Unionism; Great Depression
      b.   Industrial Revolution; Golden Age of Labor
      c.   Human Relations Movement; Industrial Revolution
      d.   Great Depression; Golden Age of Unionism

Learning Goal 4
9.   The systems approach to management was viewed as a way of
      thinking about the job of managing, providing a framework for
      visualizing _____ and _____ factors as an integrated whole.
      a.   organizational and communication
      b.   internal and external environmental
      c.   social and political
      d.   legal and political

10.   Under the systems approach, the organization can be seen as either as
      a(n) _____ where it interacts with its external environment or
      as a(n) _____ where it has no interaction with its external
      environment.
      a.   open system; closed system
      b.   interactive system; non-interactive system
      c.   closed system; open system
      d.   influential system; independent system

Learning Goal 5
11.   The controlling/authoritative manager believes that most employees
      don't like to work and will only work at the required level of
      productivity if they are forced by threat of punishment. What theory is
      this?
      a.   Theory Z
      b.   Scientific Management Theory
      c.   Theory Y
      d.   Theory X

12. _____ managers manage in a democratic and participative manner.
    a. Theory X
    b. Theory Y
    c. Scientific Management theory
    d. Contingency approach

13. Which theory attempts to integrate Japanese and American management practices?
    a. Theory X
    b. Theory Y
    c. Theory Z
    d. Contingency approach

Learning Goal 6
14. Which of these refers to different situations and conditions require different management approaches?
    a. Theory X
    b. Theory Y
    c. Theory Z
    d. Contingency approach

Learning Goal 7
15. "The excellent companies of today will not necessarily be the excellent companies of tomorrow" is a lesson learned from:
    a. Collins and Porras *Built to Last* book.
    b. Peters and Waterman's *In Search of Excellence* book.
    c. Collins' *Good to Great* book.
    d. Frederick Taylor's scientific management philosophy.

16. Fourteen of the original companies Peters and Waterman identified began to stumble, and twelve of them stumbled because:
    a. they were unable to adapt to fundamental changes in their market.
    b. they had unusual disasters occur.
    c. they had too much corporate corruption.
    d. new laws were passed by Congress.

17. American management shifted from finding and correcting mistakes or rejects to preventing them, which led to the development of:
    a. Prevention management
    b. Kaizen
    c. Total Quality Management (TQM)
    d. Hedgehog concept

Learning Goal 8
18. Based on both *In Search of Excellence* and *Built to Last*, it seems that excellence or superior vision can be very short-term commodities and that managers can never rely on their _____ to guarantee

    _____.
    a. star product; profit
    b. predictions; results
    c. strategies; improvement
    d. current successes; future successes

19. Great companies develop a simple core concept that guides all their future strategies as opposed to chasing every new management fad or policy implementation is known as the:
    a. Hedgehog concept
    b. Good to Great concept
    c. Simple concept
    d. Core Concept

TRUE-FALSE

Learning Goal 1
1. The Industrial Revolution was the move from an almost totally farming-based society to an industrialized society. T

2. Speed and efficiency dramatically decreased after the Industrial Revolution. F

3. There were four captains that shaped American business: John Rockefeller, Cornelius Vanderbilt, James Duke, and Andrew Carnegie. T

Learning Goal 2

4.   Henry Fayol is responsible for the scientific management philosophy. F

5.   The Gantt chart, invented by Frederick W. Taylor, graphically depicts
        both expected and completed production. F

6.   Douglas McGregor was the first to outline what today are called the
        functions of management. F

Learning Goal 3

7.   Mary Parker Follett had a basic theory that the fundamental problem
        of any organization was to build and maintain dynamic yet
        harmonious human relations within the organization. T

Learning Goal 4

8.   A closed system interacts with its external environment. F

Learning Goal 5

9.   Theory X and Y were described by psychologist Douglas McGregor. T

10.   Theory X suggests that employees are trustworthy, they like to work,
        and they can meet production targets on their own. F

11.   Japanese managers encouraged more employee participation in
        decision making, they showed a deeper concern for the personal well-
        being of employees, and they placed a greater emphasis on the quality
        of their products and services. T

Learning Goal 6

12.   "It all depends" describes the contingency approach to management. T

Learning Goal 7

13.   The book *In Search of Excellence* identified 36 Japanese companies
        that demonstrated excellent performance which resulted in the
        development of Theory Z. F

14.   America developed the total quality management philosophy after the
        successes of the Japanese. T

Learning Goal 8

15.   The hedgehog concept is when managers focus on simple, basic
       principles that allow the company to focus on performance rather than
       pursuing several strategic projects at the same time.

ANSWERS

LEARNING THE LANGUAGE

1. Hawthorne effect	10. Scientific management
2. Motion study	11. Contingency approach to management
3. Theory Y	12. System
4. Closed system	13. Theory X
5. Hedgehog concept	14. Functions of management
6. Industrial revolution	15. Professional manager
7. Soldiering	
8. Open system	
9. Theory Z	

ASSESSMENT CHECK

1.   Daniel Wren has described the Industrial Revolution as having three
      components. These were power, transportation, and communication.
      Power was no longer coming from horses or water; the steam engine
      and other new inventions produced more power that allowed
      industries to expand into new areas. Transportation progressed with
      ways of travel through canals, railroads, and road systems.
      Communication dramatically improved by way of the telegraph,
      telephone, and radio.

2.   The four captains and their industries were:
      John D. Rockefeller – oil
      James B. Duke – tobacco
      Andrew Carnegie – steel
      Cornelius Vanderbilt – steamships and railroads

3.   The Sherman Antitrust Act was passed in 1890 and sought to check corporate practices "in restraint of trade." The government began to regulate business and previous management methods were no longer applicable to US industry.

4.   Taylor found that employees were soldiering because workers had little or no reason to produce more. Most of the wage systems were based on attendance and position.

5.   Scientific management was based on four main principles: (1) the development of a scientific method of designing jobs to replace the old rule-of-thumb methods, (2) the scientific selection and progressive teaching and development of employees, (3) the bringing together of scientifically selected employees and scientifically developed methods for designing jobs, and (4) a division of work resulting in interdependence between management and workers.

6.   The philosophy of scientific management is about the relationship between people and work, not a technique or an efficiency device. Taylor's ideas were based on a concern not only for the proper design of the job but also for the worker.

7.   Henry Lawrence Gantt was a colleague of Frederick Taylor's at Midvale Steel and later at Bethlehem Steel. He is best know for his work in production control and his invention of the Gantt chart which graphically depicts both expected and completed production.

8.   The Hawthorne studies are generally recognized as igniting the interest of business in the human element of the workplace. The study took place in the Hawthorne plant of Western Electric. Researchers were testing the relationship between physical working conditions and worker productivity. The result was the Hawthorne Effect which states that giving special attention to a group of employees changes their behavior.

9.   Chester Barnard was the president of New Jersey Bell Telephone. He viewed an organization as a social structure and stressed the behavioral aspects of organizations.

10. There are two types of systems: open and closed systems. An open system organization is influenced by its internal and external environmental factors and then the organization influences these same factors creating a dynamic relationship. The closed system organizations do not interact with their external environments.

11. Douglas McGregor proposed a simple division of management styles that captured what he argued were fundamentally different ways of managing people. Theory X is the management of people in a controlling and authoritative manner. Theory Y is the management belief that employees are trustworthy to meet production targets; therefore, they are managed in a democratic and participative manner.

12. Theory Z was developed after Japanese companies began seeing great success with their management practices. American managers realized they could learn a great deal from the Japanese. Theory Z was developed by William Ouchi and attempts to integrate the American and the Japanese management practices.

13. The contingency approach to management theorizes that different situations and conditions require different management approaches. Contingency theories have been developed in areas such as decision making, organizational design, leadership, planning, and group behavior.

14. For a list and explanation of the 8 characteristics of excellent companies, see figure 2.4 in the text.

15. Beginning in the late 1970s, a major change took place. Rather than finding and correcting mistakes or rejects, American managers started to prevent them. This led to the development of total quality management (TQM).

16. The hedgehog concept was drawn from Isaiah Berlin's essay "The hedgehog and the Fox," in which, "The fox knows many things but the hedgehog knows only one." In terms of business, this means great companies develop a simple core concept that guides all their future strategies, as opposed to chasing every new management fad or policy implementation.

CRITICAL THINKING EXERCISES

1. Student answers will vary. They should include technology revolution, the internet and other wireless advances and how it impacts our society.

2. a. Yes
    b. Yes
    c. No
    d. No
    e. Yes
    f. Yes
    g. Yes
    h. No
    i. No
    j. No
    k. No
    l. Yes

3. a. Student answers may vary. The majority of the answers may say they worked harder when with their managers and this is because they were supervised and involved.

    b. The Hawthorne Effect is being portrayed in this example.

4. Student answers may vary. They should identify the characteristics and examples of either Theory X or Theory Y styles.

5. In the scenario, John must resort to a more Theory X style of management approach and constantly monitor Greg. However, John can resort to a Theory Y style with Tom. This is describing the contingency approach to management, which is different situations and conditions require different management approaches. Tom and Greg cannot be managed in the same manner.

6. Company B should remain successful longer because they are more innovative and have the skills to adapt to the changing market. Two lessons were learned from the companies identified in the book *In Search of Excellence:* excellent companies of today will not

necessarily be the excellent companies of tomorrow, and good management requires much more than following any one set of rules.

7.　McDonald's is best known for its hamburgers. All of the non-hamburger companies (Donato's, Boston Market, Chipotle) were taking away management's focus on what the company was built on: hamburgers. So, in order to place more attention back to the hamburgers, McDonalds sold off the "distractions." This is an example of the hedgehog concept; great companies develop a simple core concept (hamburgers) that guides all of their future strategies.

PRACTICE TEST

MULTIPLE CHOICE

1. C	11. D
2. D	12. B
3. B	13. C
4. A	14. D
5. D	15. B
6. C	16. A
7. A	17. C
8. D	18. D
9. B	19. A
10. A	

TRUE FALSE

1. True	9. True
2. False	10. False
3. True	11.True
4. False	12. False
5. False	13. False
6. False	14. True
7. True	15. True
8. False	

Chapter 3- Communication Skills

After you have read this chapter, you should be able to:

1.   Define communication and explain why effective communication is an important management skill.
2.   Describe the interpersonal communication process.
3.   Understand the importance and appropriate use of written and oral communication.
4.   Identify the best means of communication as it pertains to specific situations.
5.   Explain the most common mechanisms for communicating within the organization.
6.   Understand the challenges of communication in international business activities.

LEARNING THE LANGUAGE

Listed below are important terms found in the chapter. Choose the correct term for each definition and write it in the space provided.

Communication	Interpersonal communication
e-mail	Intranet
Grapevine	Perception
Internet	Semantics

1.   PERCEPTION _____ is the mental and sensory processes an individual uses in interpreting information received.

2.   INTERPERSONAL COMMUNICATION _____ is an interactive process between individuals that involves sending and receiving verbal and nonverbal messages.

3.   Informal channels of communication within an organization refer to GRAPEVINE

4.   The act of exchanging information is called _Communication_

5.   The _In Tranet_ is a private corporate computer network that uses Internet products and technologies to provide multimedia applications within organizations.

6.   _E-mail_ refers to the system of sending and receiving messages over an electronic communications system.

7.   The _Internet_ is a global collection of independently operating, but interconnected, computers.

8.   _Semantics_ is the science or study of the meanings of words and symbols.

ASSESSMENT CHECK

Learning Goal 1
Define communication and explain why effective communication is an important management skill.
1.   What is communication and what is it used for?

2.   Identify the reasons why communicating effectively is such an important management skill.

Learning Goal 2
Describe the interpersonal communication process.
3.   Using the figure, explain the interpersonal communication process.

4.   What is the basic purpose of interpersonal communication?

5.	What are some of the causes of interpersonal communication failure?

6.	What are the two general types of problems involved in semantics?

Learning Goal 3
Understand the importance and appropriate use of written and oral communication.
7.	Before mastering written or verbal communication, what must managers do?

8.	What are the specific questions managers must be able to answer when determining their audience?

9.	What are the steps involved in learning to actively listen?

10.	What do successful managers use oral communication skills for?

Learning Goal 4
Identify the best means of communication as it pertains to specific situations.

11.   Describe when written and oral communication is most appropriate.

Learning Goal 5
Explain the most common mechanisms for communicating within the organization.

12.   When do grapevines develop within organizations?

13.   What is the primary advantage of electronic mail systems?

14.   What is the purpose of an intranet?

Learning Goal 6
Understand the challenges of communication in international business activities.

15.   What problems exist with communication in international business activities?

16.   What two things should a manager do to improve communication internationally?

CRITICAL THINKING EXERCISES

Learning Goal 1

1.   Suppose you are a car salesman. You deal with all kinds of customers everyday. The majority of your salary is based on commission from your car sales. To be successful in this situation, how important are your communication skills and why? What are some of the skills you will need to have to help you succeed and why are they important?

Learning Goal 2

2.   Joe is the manager of a fast-food restaurant. The store is having trouble meeting its objectives, so Joe calls a staff meeting. He starts by explaining the goals and what the recent results have been. While talking, Joe looks around the room and sees that Bill is yawning, Sally is crying, and several others have totally different facial expressions.

      a.   What type of communication is Joe trying to create?
      b.   Describe what is going on with his employees.

Learning Goal 3

3.   Assume you are the manager of a construction company. Who are your different audiences? Describe a situation when you may need to use your written communication skills and when you may use your oral communication skills.

Learning Goal 4

4.   John had to fire an employee last week. He gave her three written warnings before letting her go. Was this the appropriate method of communication? Why or why not?

Learning Goal 5

5.   As a student, describe how e-mail, the internet, and the intranet have affected your life.

Learning Goal 6
6.   You are starting a granite countertop company in the United States. However, all of your suppliers are from other countries (Spain, Italy, Mexico, etc.). Describe some of the hardships that you may face when dealing with these suppliers and your plans for conquering these problems.

PRACTICE TEST

MULTIPLE CHOICE – Circle the best answer.

Learning Goal 1
1.   Communication can be used to do all of the following except:
        a.   Inform
        b.   Manufacture
        c.   Command
        d.   Influence

2.   All of the following are important management skills for communicating effectively except:
        a.   Managers must give direction to the people who work for them.
        b.   Managers must be able to absorb the ideas of others.
        c.   Managers must be able to motivate people.
        d.   Managers must be able to think critically.

3.   The basic purpose of interpersonal communication is to:
      a.   transmit information so that the sender of the message is understood and understands the response of the receiver.
      b.   transmit information across different boundaries (phone, internet, etc.).
      c.   interpret body language usage without verbally speaking.
      d.   interpret an e-mail message.

4.   Which of the following is not a cause of interpersonal communication failure?
      a.   Semantics
      b.   Poor listening habits
      c.   Reacting to a message
      d.   Emotions either preceding or during communication

5.   Good managers and salespeople always seek _____, before continuing the communication process.
      a.   only verbal feedback
      b.   only written feedback
      c.   only nonverbal feedback
      d.   both verbal and nonverbal feedback

6.   Semantics is the study of:
      a.   the tone of voice.
      b.   the meanings of words and symbols.
      c.   listening.
      d.   online communication.

Learning Goal 3
7.   In order to master verbal and written communication, managers must be able to do all of the following except:
      a.   Identify the audience.
      b.   Develop good listening skills.
      c.   Understand importance of feedback.
      d.   Read the mind of the sender.

8. Learning to listen actively involves all of the following steps except:
   a. Identify the speaker's main ideas.
   b. Identify the speaker's purpose.
   c. Tune out the tone of the speaker's voice.
   d. Respond to the speaker with appropriate comments, questions, and body language.

9. The flow from the receiver to the sender is called _____.
   a. feedback
   b. interpretation
   c. paralanguage
   d. semantics

10. All of the following are forms of nonverbal communication, except:
    a. Tone
    b. Facial expressions
    c. Words
    d. Body posture

11. All of the following are basic principles for writing effectively, except:
    a. Write as clearly as possible.
    b. Be sure that the content and tone of the document are appropriate for the audience.
    c. Proofread the document.
    d. Use large words to demonstrate intelligence.

12. Which of the following is NOT a guideline for effective oral communication?
    a. Speak slow and in a monotone.
    b. Avoid interrupting others.
    c. Avoid empty sounds or words, such as "um".
    d. Always be courteous.

Learning Goal 5
13.　Informal channels of communication within an organization are called:
　　a.　super-highways.
　　b.　tree limbs.
　　c.　grapevines.
　　d.　spider-webs.

14.　What system provides for high-speed exchange of written messages through the use of computerized text?
　　a.　Cell phones
　　b.　E-mail
　　c.　Written memo on a company letterhead
　　d.　Telepathy

Learning Goal 6
15.　All of the following are reasons that international communication becomes more complicated, except:
　　a.　Speaking different languages.
　　b.　Distance between countries.
　　c.　Cultural differences.
　　d.　Writing in different languages.

TRUE-FALSE

Learning Goal 1
1.　Managers spend as much as one-half of their time communicating.

F

2.　Managers use effective communications skills to absorb information, to motivate others, and to deal effectively with customers and coworkers.

T

Learning Goal 2
3.　Communication between individuals, especially between a manager and subordinates, is insignificant to achieving organizational objectives.

F

4.　Sound communication usually flows from ensuring that the sender and the receiver see and understand assumptions in the same way.

T

5. One problem involved in semantics is some words and phrases invite multiple interpretations. T

6. Semantics deal with the mental and sensory processes an individual uses in interpreting information she or he receives. F

Learning Goal 3

7. Good listening skills enable managers to absorb the information they need, recognize problems, and understand other people's viewpoints. T

8. Immediately after listening to a 10-minute oral presentation, the average listener has heard, comprehended, accurately evaluated, and retained about three-quarters of what was said. F

9. Feedback informs the sender whether the receiver has received the correct message. T

10. Paralanguage includes pitch, tempo, loudness, and hesitations in the verbal communication. T

11. Most oral communication is formal. F

Learning Goal 4

12. Verbal communication is most appropriate for communicating routine information. F

Learning Goal 5

13. The grapevine generally has a poor reputation because it is regarded as the primary source of distorted messages and rumors. T

14. The nonverbal communication is frequently referred to as the information super-highway. F

15. The intranet serves as an "information hub" for the entire organization. T

Learning Goal 6

16. More than 30,000 languages are spoken and about 3,000 of these are official languages of nations. F

17.   Spanish is the leading international language.

ANSWERS

LEARNING THE LANGUAGE

1. Perception	5. Intranet
2. Interpersonal Communication	6. e-mail
3. Grapevine	7. Internet
4. Communication	8. Semantics

ASSESSMENT CHECK

1.   Communications is the act of exchanging information. It can be used to inform, command, instruct, assess, influence, and persuade other people.

2.   There are five reasons why effective communication is such an important management skill:
   • Managers must give direction to the people who will work for them.
   • Managers must be able to motivate people.
   • Managers must be able to convince customers that they should do business with them.
   • Managers must be able to absorb the ideas of others.
   • Managers must be able to persuade other people.

3.   Figure 3.2 depicts the interpersonal communication process. The sender creates a message that is generated from information. This message is communicated both verbally and nonverbally. The receiver perceives the message, derives meaning, and reacts to it. The reaction creates a reply message to the sender which is communicated both verbally and non-verbally. This reply is referred to as feedback. The sender perceives the feedback and derives meaning, then reacts to the message.

4. The basic purpose of interpersonal communication is to transmit information so that the sender of the message is understood and understands the response of the receiver.

5. Some causes of interpersonal communication failure are conflicting or inappropriate assumptions, different interpretations of the meanings of words, differences in perception, emotions either preceding or during communication, poor listening habits, inadequate communication skills, insufficient feedback, and differences in the interpretations of nonverbal communications.

6. There are two general types of problems involved in semantics. The first is that some words and phrases have multiple interpretations. The second is that groups of people in specific situations often develop their own technical language, which outsiders may or may not understand.

7. Before managers can master either written or oral communication, they must be able to identify the audience, develop good listening skills, and understand the importance of feedback and non-verbal communication.

8. When determining and communicating effectively with the audience, there are specific questions managers need to be able to answer. First, what does the audience already know? What does it want to know? What is its capacity for absorbing information? What does it hope to gain by listening? Is it hoping to be motivated? Informed? Convinced? Lastly, is the audience friendly or hostile?

9. Learning to actively listen involves several steps. You must identify the speaker's purpose. Identify the speaker's main ideas. Pay attention and note the speaker's tone as well as his or her body language. Respond to the speaker with appropriate comments, questions, and body language.

10. Managers use oral communication for giving clear instructions, motivating their staff, and persuading others.

11. Verbal communication is most appropriate for sensitive communication, such as reprimanding or dismissing an employee. Written communication is most appropriate for communicating routine information, such as changes in company policies or staff.

12. Grapevines develop within organizations when employees share common hobbies, hometowns, lunch breaks, family ties, and social relationships.

13. The primary advantages of an electronic mail system is that it saves time, eliminates wasted effort, provides written records of communications without the formality of memos, and enables communication among individuals who might not communicate otherwise.

14. An intranet connects people to people and people to information and knowledge within the organization. It serves as an "information hub" for the entire organization.

15. The challenges with international communication is dealing with different languages. Another one is the cultural differences in non-verbal communication.

16. To improve the effectiveness in international communication, managers should learn the culture of the people with whom he or she communicates. They should also learn to write and speak clearly and simply.

CRITICAL THINKING EXERCISES

1. Students will have varying answers. As a car salesman with a commission-based salary, communication skills are crucial. If you do not have good communication skills, you won't sell very many cars, and, therefore, will make very little money. Some of the skills you will need as a car salesman are speaking, persuasive, motivational, and listening skills. Well-developed speaking skills are important because it portrays confidence, and clearly sends your message to potential customers. Persuasion and motivational skills will help convince these potential customers that you are the person to buy

from, not the competition down the street. Listening skills will help you understand what the customer is looking for, rather than trying to sell something that is of no use to them.

2.   a.   Joe is trying to create interpersonal communication where he interacts with his employees.

      b.   Joe is experiencing negative feedback and many of the factors that cause the interpersonal communication process to fail such as emotions, poor listening habits, different interpretations, or insufficient feedback. Effective communication is critical to achieving organizational objectives.

3.   Student answers will vary. Some of the different audiences may include employees, co-managers, suppliers, architects, engineers, surveyors, sub-contracting companies, etc. Written communication can be used for any type of routine work such as memos, reminders, e-mails, etc. Oral communication is used when you explain a job to subcontractors or when you have to reprimand an employee.

4.   John's method of three written warnings was not the appropriate method of communicating. Reprimands or warnings should start with oral so that you, as the manager, can be sure your message was clear and understood. John's employee may not have known what she was doing wrong and therefore, continued to do the same things.

5.   Student answers will vary. E-mail makes communication much faster and efficient. Notes and group projects can be set up through e-mail. The use of the internet and the intranet makes research and information much quicker and more recent and accurate.

6.   Student answers will vary. Language will be a big barrier in communicating effectively with these suppliers. Also, cultural differences will play a role. Business is run differently in different parts of the world. To help solve these problems, you should learn the culture of the people you are dealing with, and you should learn to speak and write clearly and simply.

PRACTICE TEST

MULTIPLE CHOICE

1. B	9. A
2. D	10. C
3. A	11. D
4. C	12. A
5. D	13. C
6. B	14. B
7. D	15. B
8. C	

TRUE FALSE

1. False	10. True
2. True	11. False
3. False	12. False
4. True	13. True
5. True	14. False
6. False	15. True
7. True	16. False
8. False	17. False
9. True	

Chapter 4 – Decision-Making Skills

After you have read this chapter, you should be able to:

1. Explain the difference between decision making and problem solving.
2. Compare and contrast intuitive and rational approaches to decision making.
3. Explain the decision-maker's environment and the conditions for making a decision.
4. Explain timing and participation as they relate to the decision-making process.
5. Identify methods for creative decision making.
6. Discuss management information systems.

LEARNING THE LANGUAGE

Listed below are important terms found in the chapter. Choose the correct term for each definition and write it in the space provided.

Brainstorming	Maximin approach
Brainwriting	Optimizing
Creativity	Optimizing approach
Data processing	Principle of bounded rationality
Decision making	Problem solving
Decision process	Rational approach
Gordon technique	Risk-averting approach
Innovation	Satisficing
Intuitive approach	Situation of certainty
Level of aspiration	Situation of risk
Management information system	Situation of uncertainty
Maximax approach	Transaction-processing systems

1. _Problem solving_ is the process of determining the appropriate responses or actions necessary to alleviate a problem.

2. _Optimizing Approach_ includes the following steps: recognize the need for a decision; establish rank, rank, and weigh criteria; gather available information and data; identify possible alternatives; evaluate each alternative with respect to all criteria; and select the best alternative.

3. A situation that occurs when a decision maker knows exactly what will happen and can often calculate the precise outcome for each alternative is called ___situation of certainty___

4. _Creativity_ is coming up with an idea that is new, original, useful, or satisfying to its creator or to someone else.

5. Presenting a problem to a group and allowing the group members to produce a large quantity of ideas for its solution while initially forbidding criticism refers to ___Brainstorming___

6. When managers make decisions based largely on hunches and intuition, it is called the ___intuitive approach___

7. The ___principle of bounded rationality___ assumes people have the time and cognitive ability to process only a limited amount of information on which to base decisions.

8. The ___level of aspiration___ is the level of performance that a person expects to attain; determined by the person's prior successes and failures.

9. ___situation of risk___ is a situation that occurs when a decision maker is aware of the relative probabilities of occurrence associated with each alternative.

10. The ___Decision process___ is a process that involves three stages: intelligence, design, and choice.

11. _Satisficing_ is selecting the first alternative that meets the decision maker's minimum standard of satisfaction.

12. _Optimizing_ is selecting the best possible alternative.

13. ___Decision making___ in its narrowest sense is the process of choosing from among various alternatives.

14. The _____ (Maximax approach) is selecting the alternative whose best possible outcome is the best of all possible outcomes for all alternatives; sometimes called the optimistic or gambling approach to decision making.

15. _____ (Innovation) is the process of applying a new and creative idea to a product, service, or method of operation.

16. The _____ (Gordon Technique) differs from brainstorming in that no one but the group leader knows the exact nature of the real problem under consideration. A key word is used to describe a problem area.

17. The _____ (Management information system) is an integrated approach for providing interpreted and relevant data that can help managers make decisions.

18. _____ (Transaction Processing system) substitutes computer processing for manual recordkeeping procedures.

19. _____ (Brainwriting) is a technique in which a group is presented with a problem situation and members anonymously write down ideas then exchange papers with others, who build on ideas and pass them on until all members have participated.

20. The capturing, processing, and storage of data refers to _____ (Data Processing).

21. When a decision maker has very little or no reliable information on which to evaluate the different possible outcomes, a _____ (situation of) occurs. (Uncertainty)

22. The _____ (Maximin approach) is comparing the worst possible outcomes for each alternative and selecting the one that is least undesirable; sometimes called the pessimistic approach to decision making.

23. The approach to decision making that attempts to evaluate factual information through the use of some type of deductive reasoning is called the _____ (Rational Approach)

24. The _____ (Risk Averting Approach) is choosing the alternative with the least variation among its possible outcomes.

53

Learning Goal 1
Explain the difference between decision making and problem solving.
1.   What are the three stages of the decision process described by Herbert Simon?

Inteligence, Design, choice

2.   What is the difference between decision making and problem solving?

— choosing from various alternatives

— All Actions necessary to avert the problem.

Learning Goal 2
Compare and contrast intuitive and rational approaches to decision making.
3.   What are the emotional attachments that can hurt decision makers?

Hunches & intuition

4.   What are Ordiorne's two suggestions for managers and decision makers overwhelmed by emotional attachments?

Fastining on unsubstantiate facts & sticking with them.

Pressing every fact into a mega pattern.

5.   What are the steps involved in the optimizing approach to decision making?

1. Recoginize need for decision.
2. Establish rank & weigh
3. Gather available info & data.
4. Identify possibe alternatives.
5. Evaluate each alternative.
6. Select the best.

6. What does the principle of bounded rationality state?

The capacity of human mind for formulating & solving complex problems is very small compared with the size of problem.

Learning Goal 3

Explain the decision maker's environment and the conditions for making a decision.

7. Name the major environmental factors influencing decision makers in an organization.

8. What is the difference between certainty, risk, and uncertainty?

Learning Goal 4

Explain timing and participation as they relate to the decision-making process.

9. Describe the implications of making quick decisions.

10. Why is group performance generally superior to that of the average group member?

Learning Goal 5
Identify methods for creative decision making.
11.   What are the four basic barriers to effective decision making?

12.   What is the difference between creativity and innovation?

13.   What must managers do to avoid hindering creativity?

Learning Goal 6
Discuss management information systems.
14.   What is data processing?

15.   What are transaction-processing systems? Name some examples.

CRITICAL THINKING EXERCISES

Learning Goal 1
1.   Suppose you are the vice president of security in a casino. You have important decisions to make and problems to solve. Explain some of these problems and the decisions that you would make when faced with those situations.

Learning Goal 2
2.   Assume you are a financial manager for a manufacturing firm. Is it best to make decisions using an intuitive approach, optimizing approach, or satisficing approach? Name some of the implications of each approach.

Learning Goal 3
3.   Assume you are the manager of a residential construction company. What are the environmental factors that would affect your decisions?

4.   As the general manager, do you feel that an organization will be more successful with a management team making decisions or with the manager for each department making decisions on their own? Why or why not?

Learning Goal 5
5.   Creativity and innovation are important for continuous success. What are some of the things you would do to encourage creativity and an innovative environment? Why would you use these techniques?

PRACTICE TEST

MULTIPLE CHOICE – Circle the best answer.

Learning Goal 1
1.   Decision making encompasses all the basic management functions, which are:
    a.   planning, organizing, staffing, leading, and controlling.
    b.   planning, regulating, supervising, and networking.
    c.   supervising, networking, patrolling, and staffing.
    d.   formulating, implementing, evaluating, and controlling.

2. Which of these best describe problem solving?
   a. A deviation from some standard or desired level of performance.
   b. The process of choosing from among various alternatives.
   c. The process of determining the appropriate responses or actions necessary to alleviate a problem.
   d. A process that involves three stages: intelligence, design, and choice.

Learning Goal 2
3. When a manager makes decisions solely on hunches or feelings, they are using which of these?
   a. Rational approach
   b. Intuitive approach
   c. Decision process
   d. Optimizing approach

4. All of the following are emotional attachments that can hurt decision makers, except:
   a. Being attracted to scandalous issues and heightening their significance.
   b. Reviewing all relevant data and evaluating alternatives.
   c. Overlooking everything except what is immediately useful.
   d. Fastening on unsubstantiated facts and sticking with them.

5. Which of the following is NOT a step in the optimizing approach to decision making?
   a. Select the best alternative
   b. Identify possible alternatives
   c. Recognize the need for a decision
   d. Ignore gossip and hearsay

6. Satisficing means:
   a. selecting the best possible alternative.
   b. sacrificing in order to satisfy the objective.
   c. selecting the first alternative that meets the decision maker's minimum standard of satisfaction.
   d. lowering standards to choose first alternative.

7.   Which is NOT a major environmental factor that influences decision making in an organization?
   a.   Stock market analysts
   b.   Organizational groups
   c.   Personal traits
   d.   Individuals with the organization

8.   If certain reliable but incomplete information is available, a decision maker is in a:
   a.   situation of uncertainty.
   b.   situation of risk.
   c.   situation of certainty.
   d.   situation of danger.

9.   In a situation of certainty, the decision maker:
   a.   can rely on their intuition to guide them.
   b.   can hope the predictions are accurate.
   c.   can calculate the precise outcome for each alternative.
   d.   will choose the decision based on historical data.

10.   Also called the gambling approach, _____ approach is to choose the alternative whose best possible outcome is the best of all possible outcomes for all alternatives.
   a.   Maximin
   b.   Uncertainty
   c.   Risk-averting
   d.   Maximax

Learning Goal 4

11.   All of these are true in regards to the better decision-making skills of groups, except:
   a.   Groups contain greater knowledge.
   b.   When avoiding mistakes is more important than speed.
   c.   When speed is an issue.
   d.   The group has a much wider range of alternatives.

12. "More polar" means:
    a. that groups tend to make decisions that are more rational than those they would make as individuals.
    b. that groups tend to make decisions that are more extreme than those they would make as individuals.
    c. that groups tend to hesitate and continuously review information rather than making a decision.
    d. that groups cannot come to an agreement to make a decision.

Learning Goal 5
13. Which of the following is NOT part of the five-step process to help establish an environment for creative decision making?
    a. Substitution
    b. Illumination
    c. Verification
    d. Preparation

14. To avoid hindering creativity, managers must do all of the following except:
    a. Develop effective internal and external communication.
    b. Seek a mix of talent within the organization.
    c. Instill trust.
    d. Continue tradition with a strict organizational structure.

15. Which of the following is NOT a tool used to foster creativity?
    a. Brainstorming
    b. Brainwriting
    c. Gordon Technique
    d. Satisficing

16. All of the following are stages of the creative decision making model except:
    a. Fact finding
    b. Recognition
    c. Determination
    d. Acceptance finding

Learning Goal 6
17. The information made available by an MIS is in the following forms, except:
   a. Special reports
   b. News reports
   c. Periodic reports
   d. Outputs of mathematical simulations

TRUE-FALSE

Learning Goal 1
1. To be a good planner, organizer, staffer, leader, and controller, a manager must first be a good decision maker.

2. Managerial decisions rarely involve solving or avoiding problems.

Learning Goal 2
3. Managers sometimes become so emotionally attached to certain positions that almost nothing will change their minds.

4. Approaches to decision making that attempt to evaluate factual information through the use of some type of deductive reasoning are referred to as intuitive approaches.

5. The intuitive approach is an improvement over the optimizing approach, but it is not without problems and limitations.

6. Level of aspiration refers to the level of performance a person expects to attain, and it is impacted by the person's prior successes and failures.

Learning Goal 3
7. Successful managers must develop an appreciation for the different environmental forces that both influence them and are influenced by their decisions.

8. Decisions are made often in today's organization under a condition of certainty.

9. F Under conditions of uncertainty, the decision maker can use expected value analysis to help arrive at a decision.

10. T There are three approaches for dealing with uncertainty: maximax, maximin, and risk-averse.

Learning Goal 4
11. T Group performance is frequently better than that of the average group member.

12. T Individuals often take longer to solve problems than does a group.

13. F Experiments have shown that unanimous group decisions are consistently riskier than the average of the individual decisions.

Learning Goal 5
14. T The challenge for today's managers is to establish an environment that encourages creativity instead of innovation.

15. T The single most important factor that influences creativity and innovation by organizational members is the climate, or environment, in which they work.

16. F Frederick Taylor developed brainstorming as an aid to producing creative ideas for an advertising agency.

Learning Goal 6
17. T MIS's are designed to produce information needed for the successful management of a process, department, or business.

18. T Data processing is the capture, processing, and storage of data, whereas an MIS uses those data to produce information for management in making decisions to solve problems.

ANSWERS

LEARNING THE LANGUAGE

1. Problem solving	13. Decision making
2. Optimizing approach	14. Maximax approach
3. Situation of certainty	15. Innovation
4. Creativity	16. Gordon technique
5. Brainstorming	17. Management information system
6. Intuitive approach	18. Transaction-processing systems
7. Principle of bounded rationality	19. Brainwriting
8. Level of aspiration	20. Data processing
9. Situation of risk	21. Situation of uncertainty
10. Decision process	22. Maximin approach
11. Satisficing	23. Rational approach
12. Optimizing	24. Risk-averting approach

ASSESSMENT CHECK

1. Herbert Simon, a Nobel Prize winner, has described the manager's decision process in three stages: 1) intelligence, 2) design, and 3) choice.

2. Decision making is the process of choosing from among various alternatives. Problem solving is the process of determining the appropriate responses or actions necessary to alleviate a problem.

3. There are five emotional attachments that George Odiorne believes can hurt a decision maker:
   1) Fastening on unsubstantiated facts and sticking with them.
   2) Being attracted to scandalous issues and heightening their significance.
   3) Pressing every fact into a moral pattern.
   4) Overlooking everything except what is immediately useful.
   5) Having a preference for romantic stories and finding such information more significant than any other kind, including hard evidence.

4. The first suggestion is to become aware of biases and allow for them. The second is to seek independent opinions.

5. 1) Recognize the need for a decision.
   2) Establish, rank, and weigh the decision criteria.
   3) Gather available information and data.
   4) Identify possible alternatives.
   5) Evaluate each alternative with respect to all criteria.
   6) Select the best alternative.

6. The principle of bounded rationality states, "The capacity of the human mind for formulating and solving complex problems is very small compared with the size of the problems whose solution is required for objectively rational behavior – or even for a reasonable approximation to such objective rationality." It is simply stating that human rationality has definite limits.

7. Refer to Figure 4.2. There are organizational groups such as advisory committees, labor unions, and informal groups. There are individuals within the organization such as subordinates and superiors. Personality traits such as personality, background, and experience affect decisions as well. The organization itself has an affect too. The position, structure, purpose, and the traditions of the organization have an impact on the decisions that are made.

8. A situation of certainty is knowing exactly what will happen. A situation of risk occurs when if certain reliable but incomplete information is available. A situation of uncertainty is when there is very little or no reliable information on which to evaluate different possible outcomes.

9. A manager who makes quick decisions is taking a risk of making bad decisions because they have not gathered and evaluated the available data, considered people's feelings, and anticipated the impact of the decision which can result in a quick but poor decision.

10. There are two reasons why group performance is generally superior to that of the average group member. First, the sum total of the group's

knowledge is greater. Second, the group has a much wider range of alternatives in the decision process.

11.   The first barrier is complacency. The second is called defensive avoidance and the third is panic. The last barrier is deciding to decide.

12.   Creativity is coming up with an idea that is new, original, useful, or satisfying to its creator or to someone else. Innovation is the process of applying a new and creative idea to a product, service, or method of operation.

13.   Managers must instill trust and eliminate the fear of failure. They must develop effective internal and external communication. Also, they must seek a mix of talent within the organization. This will blend different personality types and interactions which encourages creative problem solving. Managers should reward useful ideas and solutions. Lastly, they should allow for some flexibility in the existing organizational structure so that new ideas and creative solutions will not be eliminated by tradition.

14.   Data processing is the capture, processing, and storage of data, whereas an MIS uses those data to produce information for management in making decisions to solve problems. Data processing provides the database of the MIS.

15.   Transaction-processing systems substitute computer processing for manual record-keeping procedures. They require routine and highly structured decisions. Some examples include payroll, billing, and inventory record systems.

CRITICAL THINKING EXERCISES

1.   Students will have varying answers. When in charge of security, one must deal with people that are "causing a scene" or belligerent individuals. They also have problems of theft, securing the property and people, and must make decisions regarding how to deal with these issues.

2.   Students may offer different answers. The optimizing approach would be the obvious answer because all factors must be researched and considered, not chosen solely on feelings. Also, satisficing is never the best approach because patience will allow for a better alternative when time is not critical.

3.   Students answers will vary. Many factors would affect the decisions that are made. These include superiors, employees, purpose of the company, tradition, structure, experience in the industry, etc.

4.   Students answers will vary. Groups are almost always the better way to go, unless time is of the essence.

5.   Students answers will vary. Innovation and creativity can be created through a variety of techniques. Brainstorming, brainwriting, and the Gordon technique are all techniques discussed in the chapter. For example, 3M, manufacturer of Scotch Tapes and Post-It Note Pads, gives its employees time in their workday strictly for creating new products.

PRACTICE TEST

MULTIPLE CHOICE

1. A	10. D
2. C	11. C
3. B	12. B
4. B	13. A
5. D	14. D
6. C	15. D
7. A	16. C
8. B	17. B
9. C	

TRUE FALSE

1. True	10. True
2. False	11. True
3. True	12. False
4. False	13. True
5. False	14. False
6. True	15. True
7. True	16. False
8. False	17. True
9. False	18. True

Chapter 5 – Planning and Strategic Management

After you have read this chapter, you should be able to:

1. Define planning and distinguish between formal and functional plans.
2. Contrast strategic planning with operational planning.
3. Define the Management By Objectives (MBO) Process.
4. Define strategy and explain the strategic management process.
5. Define organizational mission and explain how mission relates to long- and short-range objectives.
6. Discuss the components of a SWOT analysis.

LEARNING THE LANGUAGE

Listed below are important terms found in the chapter. Choose the correct term for each definition and write it in the space provided.

Business strategies	Mission
Combination strategies	Objectives
Contingency plans	Operations planning
Corporate strategies	Planning
Defensive or retrenchment strategies	Policies
Evaluation phase	Procedure
External environment	Rules
Formal plan	Short-range objectives
Formulation phase	Short-range plans
Functional plans	Stability strategies
Functional strategies	Strategic business unit
Grand strategies	Strategic management
Growth strategies	Strategic planning
Implementation phase	Strategy
Long-range objectives	SWOT
Long-range plans	Tactical planning
Management by objectives (MBO)	

1.	The _____ is a distinct business that has its own set of competitors and can be managed reasonably independently of other businesses within the organization.

2.	_____ consists of everything outside the organization.

3.	_____ is formulation, proper implementation, and continuous evaluation of strategic plans.

4.	_____ are broad, general guides to action that constrain or direct objective attainment.

5.	_____ is a philosophy based on converting organizational objectives into personal objectives. It assumes that establishing personal objectives elicits employee commitment, which leads to improved performance.

6.	_____ focus on how to compete in a given business.

7.	_____ goes beyond the current fiscal year. They must support and not conflict with the organizational mission.

8.	A(n) _____ is a written, documented plan developed through an identifiable process.

9.	The process of deciding what objectives to pursue during a future time period and what to do to achieve those objectives is called _____.

10.	_____ is concerned with the activities of the different functional areas of the business.

11.	The _____ defines the basic purpose of an organization; why the organization exists.

12.	_____ is an acronym for strengths, weaknesses, opportunities, and threats.

13. _____ originate from functional areas of an organization such as production, marketing, finance, and personnel.

14. The _____ is the third phase in strategic management, in which the implemented strategic plan is monitored, evaluated, and updated.

15. _____ generally covers up to one-year.

16. _____ address what-ifs of the manager's job; get the manager in the habit of being prepared and knowing what to do if something does go wrong.

17. _____ is short-term planning and concentrates on the formulation of functional plans.

18. _____ are generally tied to a specific time period of a year or less and are derived from an in-depth evaluation of long-range objectives.

19. A(n) _____ is a series of related steps or task expressed in chronological order for a specific purpose.

20. _____ outlines the basic steps management plans to take to reach an objective or a set of objectives.

21. _____ are used when the organization tries to expand, as measured by sales, product line, number of employees, or similar measures.

22. Specific and definite actions to be taken or not to be taken in a given situation are called _____.

23. _____ is the first phase in strategic management, in which the initial strategic plan is developed.

24. _____ are used when the organization is satisfied with its present course.

25. _____ typically span at least three to five years; some extend as far as 20 years into the future.

26. _____ is the same as operations planning; it concentrates on the formulation of functional plans and done primarily by middle to lower-level managers.

27. _____ address which businesses an organization will be in and how resources will be allocated among those businesses.

28. _____ is the second phase in strategic management, in which the strategic plan is put into effect.

29. _____ are used when a company wants or needs to reduce its operations.

30. Corporate strategies are sometimes called _____.

31. The application of the basic planning process at the highest levels of the organization is called _____. It determines the long-run directions and performance of an organization.

32. _____ are used when an organization simultaneously employs different strategies for different parts of the company.

33. _____ are statements outlining what the organization is trying to achieve; they give an organization and its members direction.

ASSESSMENT CHECK

Learning Goal 1
Define planning and distinguish between formal and functional plans.
1. What are the positive effects of planning on managerial performance?

2. What is the difference between formal plans and functional plans?

Learning Goal 2
Contrast strategic planning with operational planning.
3.   What is the major difference between strategic and operational
      planning?

4.   Describe the difference between short-range, intermediate, and long-
      range plans?

Learning Goal 3
Define the Management By Objectives (MBO) Process.
5.   What are objectives and what is there purpose?

6.   In organization, what are the areas in which objectives should be
      established?

7.   Describe management by objectives. What else is this philosophy
      called?

8.   What is the difference between policies, rules, and procedures?

Learning Goal 4
Define strategy and explain the strategic management process.
9.   What are the four types of corporate strategies?

10.   Name and describe the three types of business strategies.

11.   How does successful strategic management involve different levels of the organization?

Learning Goal 5
Define organizational mission and explain how mission relates to long- and short-range objectives.
12.   What is a mission statement and why is it important?

Learning Goal 6
Discuss the components of a SWOT analysis.
13.   What are the benefits of using a SWOT analysis?

CRITICAL THINKING EXERCISES

Learning Goal 1
1.   John is the manager of ABC Corp. He thinks of various plans and
        keeps them in his head. He never writes anything down or discusses
        the plans with anyone until after he makes final decisions. What are
        the implications of and problems that John may face?

Learning Goal 2
2.   Based on what news events you may have heard or read about in
        newspapers and magazines, give some examples of strategic planning
        and tactical planning.

Learning Goal 3

3.   You are on the management team of XYZ Corp. Recently, employee performance and morale has been low. You and your team want to change the style of management to attempt to motivate your workers. You want to implement management by objectives. Your boss asks you to explain what it is and how would you go about implementing the program. What would you tell him/her?

Learning Goal 4

4.   You are in the top management position at Harley Davidson (H-D). Propose some of your own strategies for H-D and your rationale explaining why.

Learning Goal 5
5. Walt Disney's mission statement is simply "To make People Happy." If you were to revise this mission statement for Walt Disney, what aspects would you add? Propose a revised mission for Disney.

Learning Goal 6
6. Develop a SWOT analysis for any your college.

PRACTICE TEST

MULTIPLE CHOICE – Circle the best answer.

Learning Goal 1
1.   Planning enables a manager to:
    a.   accept the future.
    b.   guarantee success.
    c.   affect the future rather than accept it.
    d.   focus on his/her personal goals.

2.   All of the following are types of functional plans, except:
    a.   Sales and marketing plans
    b.   New Year's Eve plans
    c.   Personnel plans
    d.   Production plans

Learning Goal 2
3.   What is the typical time span of long-range plans?
    a.   3-5 years
    b.   over 1 year
    c.   2-3 years
    d.   25 years

4.   Tactical planning focuses on the formulation of:
    a.   long range plans.
    b.   contingency plans.
    c.   functional plans.
    d.   strategic plans.

5.   A contingency plan is a:
    a.   backup plan.
    b.   primary plan.
    c.   tactical plan.
    d.   strategic plan.

6.   A key for organizational success is:
   a.   to copy the objectives and goals of competitors.
   b.   to adopt a traditional plan and keep using it.
   c.   for each department to have independent objectives.
   d.   for the objectives at all different levels to mesh together.

7.   Which of the following is NOT one of the general categories for objectives?
   a.   Profit-oriented
   b.   Historical
   c.   Social responsibility
   d.   Employee needs and well-being

8.   Management by objectives works best when the objectives of each organizational unit are derived from:
   a.   the societal environment.
   b.   the objectives of a competitor.
   c.   the objectives of the next higher unit in the organization.
   d.   the general manager.

9.   Defensive strategies consist of all of the following, except for:
   a.   Turnaround
   b.   Divestiture
   c.   Liquidation
   d.   Diversification

10.   Overall cost leadership is a strategy designed to:
   a.   produce and deliver the product or service for a lower cost than the competition.
   b.   make the product or service unique in its category.
   c.   reverse a negative trend and get the company back to profitability.
   d.   sell part of its business.

11. Which of the following is not a phase of the strategic management process?
   a. Formulation
   b. Evaluation
   c. Implementation
   d. Estimation

Learning Goal 5
12. An organization's mission is actually the:
   a. narrowest focus of the objectives.
   b. broadest and highest level of objectives.
   c. purpose determined by its customers.
   d. statement that changes with the organization's strategies.

13. Objectives cannot be accurately established without:
   a. determining threats and competition.
   b. finding opportunities for the company.
   c. examining the internal and external environments.
   d. examining similar industries and their successes.

Learning Goal 6
14. SWOT is an acronym that stands for:
   a. strategies, wealth, opportunities, threats.
   b. stakeholders, weaknesses, objectives, tactics.
   c. substitutes, weaknesses, objectives, tactics.
   d. strengths, weaknesses, opportunities, and threats.

15. Which of the following is NOT a part of the five forces model?
   a. Partners
   b. Suppliers
   c. Buyers
   d. Substitutes

TRUE-FALSE

Learning Goal 1
1. Planning provides a means for actively involving all personnel from all areas of the organization in the management of the organization.

2.	Most planning is carried out on a formal (written document) basis.

3.	Many functional plans are interrelated and interdependent.

Learning Goal 2
4.	Usually intermediate plans are derived from short-range plans, and long-range plans are derived from intermediate plans.

5.	Strategic planning is done by managers at all levels in the organization.

6.	Contingency plans address the what-ifs of the manager's job.

Learning Goal 3
7.	Long-range objectives must support and not conflict with the organizational mission.

8.	MBO works best when the objectives of each organizational unit are derived from the objectives of the unit below in the organization.

9.	Policies establish boundaries within which organizational members must operate.

10.	Unlike rules, procedures do not have to specify sequence.

Learning Goal 4
11.	A strategy outlines how management intends to achieve its objectives.

12.	A grand strategy is used when the organization is trying to expand in terms of sales, product line, number of employees, or similar measures.

13.	Stability strategies are used when an organization is not satisfied with its present course.

14.	Focus is type of business strategy where the companies direct their attention towards a narrow market segment.

15. The formulation phase stresses the importance of continuously evaluating and updating the strategic plan after it has been implemented.

Learning Goal 5
16. A mission statement usually includes a description of the organization's basic products or services.

17. Past strategies used by the organization can and should be disregarded.

18. Long-range objectives should derive from the mission statement.

Learning Goal 6
19. The SWOT analysis is a technique for evaluating an organization's strategies, weaknesses, objectives, and tactics.

20. A strategic business unit is a distinct business that has its own set of competitors and can be managed reasonably independently of other businesses within the organization.

ANSWERS

LEARNING THE LANGUAGE

1. Strategic business unit (SBU)	18. Short-range objectives
2. External environment	19. Procedure
3. Strategic Planning	20. Strategy
4. Policies	21. Growth strategies
5. Management By Objectives (MBO)	22. Rules
6. Business Strategies	23. Formulation phase
7. Long-range objectives	24. Stability strategies
8. Formal plan	25. Long-range plans
9. Planning	26. Tactical planning
10. Functional planning	27. Corporate strategies
11. Mission	28. Implementation phase
12. SWOT	29. Defensive or retrenchment strategies
13. Functional plans	30. Grand strategies
14. Evaluation phase	31. Strategic management
15. Short-range plans	32. Combination strategies
16. Contingency plans	33. Objectives
17. Operations planning	

ASSESSMENT CHECK

1. Studies have demonstrated that employees who stress planning earn high performance ratings from supervisors. They have also shown that planning has a positive impact on the quality of work produced.

2. Formal plans are written documents developed through an identifiable process. Functional plans are plans originated from functional areas such as sales and marketing, production, etc.

3. The major difference is the level at which the planning is done. Strategic planning is done primarily by top-level managers; whereas, operational planning is done by managers at all levels in the organization.

4. Short-range plans generally cover up to one year. Long-range plans span at least three to five years, with some extending as far as 20 years into the future. Intermediate plans cover the time span between short-range and long-range plans.

5. Objectives are statements outlining what the organization is trying to achieve. The purpose of objectives is to give the organization and its member's direction and purpose.

6. Objectives should be established in profitability, markets, productivity, product, financial resources, physical facilities, research and innovation, organization structure, human resources, and social responsibility.

7. Management by objectives is a philosophy based on converting organizational objectives into personal objectives. It assumes that establishing personal objectives elicits employee commitment, which leads to improved performance. MBO is also called management by results, goals and control, work planning and review, and goals management.

8. Policies are broad, general guides to action that constrain or direct objectives attainment. Rules require specific and definite actions to be taken or not to be taken in a given situation. Procedures are a series of related steps or tasks expressed in chronological order for a specific purpose.

9. The four types of corporate strategies are growth, stability, defensive or retrenchment, and combination strategies.

10. Overall cost leadership is a business strategy designed to produce and deliver the product or service for a lower cost than the competition. Differentiation is another business strategy that aims to make the product or service unique in its category, allowing the organization to charge higher-than-average prices. Focus is the last type of business strategy. Companies used this strategy to direct their attention to a narrow market segment.

11. Strategic management is guided by top management; however, successful strategic management involves many different levels in the

organization. Top level management may ask middle- and lower-level managers for input when formulating top-level plans.

12. A mission statement usually includes a description of the organization's basic products or services and a definition of its markets or sources of revenue. It defines the basic purpose or purposes of the organization. It is important because it lets all stakeholders know the organization's reason for existence.

13. The SWOT analysis provides a general overview of whether the overall situation is healthy or unhealthy. It identifies the internal strengths and weaknesses of a company, plus the external threats and opportunities that the company is faced with.

CRITICAL THINKING EXERCISES

1. Student answers will vary. Planning doesn't necessarily always have to be formal (written). However, planning enables a manager to affect the future. John is trying to make plans independently. If he doesn't seek help and cooperation within his organization the results will not be positive. John will not have a goal to reach if it's simply "in his head." He is much more likely to sit back and let things happen, and then try to react when it will be too late.

2. Student answers will vary. Mergers and acquisitions are long-range plans and would be considered strategic. Tactical planning focuses on the short-range plans of the company such as production efficiency, downsizing, rightsizing, outsourcing, etc.

3. Student answers will vary. Management by objectives is a management philosophy based on converting organizational objectives into personal objectives. Therefore, if the success of the corporation objectives directly affects the success of personal objectives, then there should be higher employee commitment and improved performance.

4. Student answers will vary. Some strategies may include moving into the customization of motorcycles, expanding into agriculture machinery, acquiring competitors, etc.

5. Student answers will vary. Some aspects that should be included are description of products and services, sources of revenue, definition of its markets, who the customers are and what they buy, and the company's values and philosophy.

6. Student answers will vary.

PRACTICE TEST

MULTIPLE CHOICE

1. C	9. D
2. B	10. A
3. A	11. D
4. C	12. B
5. A	13. C
6. D	14. D
7. B	15. A
8. C	

TRUE FALSE

1. True	11. True
2. False	12. False
3. True	13. False
4. False	14. True
5. False	15. False
6. True	16. True
7. True	17. False
8. False	18. True
9. True	19. False
10. False	20. True

Chapter 6 – Leadership and Culture

LEARNING GOALS

After you have read this chapter, you should be able to:

1. Define leadership, power, and authority.
2. Discuss leadership as it relates to management.
3. Explain leadership attitudes.
4. Describe the differences between a Theory X and Theory Y manager.
5. Explain the differences between Transactional, Transformational, and Charismatic leadership styles.
6. Identify strategies for effectively managing corporate culture.

LEARNING THE LANGUAGE

Listed below are important terms found in the chapter. Choose the correct term for each definition and write it in the space provided.

Authority	Managerial grid
Autocratic leader	Path-goal theory of leadership
Bet-your-company culture	Position power
Charismatic leadership	Power
Consideration	Process culture
Contingency approach to leadership	Self-fulfilling prophecy
Corporate culture	Situational leadership theory
Culture	Task structure
Democratic leader	Theory X
Entry socialization	Theory Y
Initiating structure	Tough-person, macho culture
Laissez-faire leader	Trait theory
Leader	Transactional leadership
LBDQ	Transformational leadership
Leader-member relations	Work-hard/ play-hard culture
Leadership	

1. A(n) _____ guides and encourages the group to make decisions.

2. According to the _____, as the followers' level of maturity of increases, structure should be reduced; while socio-emotional support should first be increased and then gradually decreased.

3. _____ is the ability to influence, command, or apply force. It is a measure of a person's potential to get others to do what he or she wants them to do, as well as to avoid being forced by others to do what he or she does not want to do.

4. _____ communicates how people in an organization should behave by establishing a value system conveyed through rites, rituals, myths, legends, and actions.

5. The _____ is a questionnaire designed to determine what a successful leader does regardless of the type of group being led.

6. _____ involves low risk with little feedback; employees focus on how things are done rather than on the outcomes.

7. A(n) _____ is one who obtains followers and influences them in setting and achieving objectives.

8. The _____ attempts to define the relationships between a leader's behavior and the subordinates' performances and work activities.

9. _____ is the power and influence that go with a job.

10. A set of important understandings (often unstated) that members of a community share is called _____.

11. _____ takes the approach that leaders engage in bargaining relationship with their followers.

12. _____ is the legitimate exercise of power. It is the right to issue directives and to expend resources; related to power but narrower in scope.

13. A(n) _____ leader would most likely use a more authoritarian style of leadership.

14. A leader behavior of showing concern for individual group members and satisfying their needs refers to _____.

15. _____ involves a leader who can successfully influence employee behavior on the strength of personality or a perceived charisma, without the formal power or experience to back it up.

16. The relationship between a leader's expectations and the resulting performance of subordinates refers to _____.

17. The _____ is a two-dimensional framework rating a leader on the basis of concern for people and concern for production.

18. The ability to influence people to willingly follow one's guidance or adhere to one's decisions is called _____.

19. _____ refers to the degree to which job tasks are structured.

20. _____ involves cultivating employee acceptance of the group mission.

21. The _____ theorizes that different situations and conditions require different management approaches.

22. _____ is leader behavior of structuring the work of group members and directing the group toward the attainment of the group's goals.

23. _____ stresses what the leader was like rather than what the leader did.

24. The _____ encourages employees to take few risks and to expect rapid feedback.

25. An adaptation process by which new employees are introduced and indoctrinated into the organization is called _____.

26. A(n) _____ makes most decisions for the group.

27. A(n) _____ leader believes that the expenditure of physical and mental effort in work is as natural as play or rest and that commitment to objectives is a function of the rewards associated with their achievement.

28. The _____ requires big-stakes decisions; considerable time passes before the results are known.

29. A(n) _____ allows people within the group to make all decisions.

30. The _____ is characterized by individuals who take high risks and get quick feedback on whether their decisions are right or wrong.

31. The degree to which others trust and respect the leader and the leader's friendliness refers to _____.

ASSESSMENT CHECK

Learning Goal 1
Define leadership, power, and authority.
1. Does power have a positive or negative connotation in today's world? Explain the forms that power can take.

2. What are the five sources of power?

Learning Goal 2
Discuss leadership as it relates to management.
3. Are leadership and management the same? Explain.

Learning Goal 3
Explain leadership attitudes.
4.   Describe the leadership attitude termed Theory X.

5.   Describe the leadership attitude termed Theory Y.

Learning Goal 4
Describe the differences between a Theory X and Theory Y manager.
6.   What are the differences between a Theory X and Theory Y manager?

Learning Goal 5
Explain the differences between Transactional, Transformational, and Charismatic leadership styles.
7.   What would a leader do under the transactional leadership approach?

8.   Describe the manager-employee relationship under transformational leadership.

9.   Why are charismatic leaders considered heroic?

Learning Goal 6
Identify strategies for effectively managing corporate culture.
10.   What are the two basic components of culture?

11.   Describe a strong and a weak corporate culture.

12.   What are the five reasons that justify a large-scale cultural change?

CRITICAL THINKING EXERCISES

Learning Goal 1
1.   Upon graduation you receive a management position at a retail store. What are the five sources of power and which ones will you likely utilize in your position. Explain why you think those sources of power will work best for you?

Learning Goal 2

2.	If you have or previously had a job or an internship, evaluate your manager's actions using the description of management behavior in this section. For example, does/did your manager tell you what to do, or does/did he or she place more emphasis on training you to make decisions on the job? Does/did management emphasize teamwork and cooperation? Has/had this manager been with the company for a long time, or has/had he or she moved around from one company to another? Is your manager a skilled communicator, team player, planner, coordinator, organizer?

Learning Goal 4

3.	Douglas McGregor developed two attitude profiles about the basic nature of people that he termed: Theory X and Theory Y. Determine which theory is portrayed in the following assumptions?

A.	_____	Under conditions of modern industrial life, the intellectual potential of the average human being is only partially utilized.

B.	_____	Commitment to objectives is a function of the rewards associated with their achievement.

C. _____ The average human being prefers to be directed, wishes to avoid responsibility, has relatively little ambition, and wants security above all.

D. _____ The average human being learns, under proper conditions, not only to accept but to seek responsibility.

E. _____ The capacity to exercise a relatively high degree of imagination, ingenuity, and creativity in the solution of organizational problems is widely, not narrowly, distributed in the population.

F. _____ The average human being has an inherent dislike of work and will avoid it if possible.

Learning Goal 5

4. You have been hired to be a supervisor in the Sun-2-Shade plant where they are going to make self-darkening windshields. Your workers are well-educated and highly skilled. How do you intend to lead and organize these employees? How will your leading (or directing) differ from that of the top manager?

5. Effective leadership styles range along a continuum based upon the amount of employee involvement in setting objectives and making decisions. The three basic leadership styles are called:

Autocratic   *Democratic*   *Laissez-Faire*

Which of those styles are being illustrated in the following situations?

A. Production workers complain about having to punch a time clock each day.

    a._____   "Too bad, I'm not getting rid of it!"

    b._____   "Let's get a committee together and see if we can come up with some alternatives to using the time clock."

B. A university sees a need for some action to be taken to reverse declining enrollment trends.

    a._____   "Let's form a committee of faculty and administrators to study the problem and give recommendations on how to solve the problem."

    b._____   "The objective for each division is to increase enrollment by 10% for the next school year. Each division is free to take whatever action is appropriate for their area in order to reach the objective."

C. A manager notices that an employee consistently turns in work past the deadline.

    a._____   "Bob, your work has been late three times this month. This is a problem. How can we work together to solve it?"

    b._____   "Bob, your work has been late three times this month. One more time and you will be disciplined. Two times and you're fired. Got it?"

6.   You have been in your supervisory position for several months, and have found your boss to be a great person with whom to work. She speaks often about the kind of division she wants to create, where all the employees feel a sense of loyalty to a team. She stresses customer service, high product quality, and fair treatment of her employees. If she makes a mistake, she is always up front about it. She insists on honesty from her employees, and you notice that all her employees are treated fairly and with respect. She expects a lot from you and her other subordinates, but is sure to let you make your own decisions (as well as you own mistakes). She encourages employee problem solving and is quick to implement changes, which makes the division more effective and efficient. What type of leadership style is your boss utilizing and in what ways is your boss creating a corporate culture?

PRACTICE TEST

MULTIPLE CHOICE – Circle the best answer.

Learning Goal 1
1. Negative power results when:
    a. the exchange is voluntary.
    b. the individual is forced to change.
    c. both parties feel good about the exchange.
    d. Power only has positive results.

2. The amount of authority a manager has depends on the amount of all the following, except:
    a. Coercive power
    b. Reward power
    c. Legitimate power
    d. Referent power

3. Leadership is:
    a. the right to issue directives and expend resources.
    b. the ability to influence, command, or apply force.
    c. the ability to influence people to willingly follow one's guidance or adhere to one's decision.
    d. the measure of a person's potential to get others to do willingly or unwillingly what he or she wants them to do.

Learning Goal 2
4. Effective leadership in organizations performs all of the following except:
    a. Formulate a disciplinary procedure for self-managed employees.
    b. Develops a strategy for moving toward that vision.
    c. Creates a vision of the future that considers the legitimate long-term interests of the parties involved in the organization.
    d. Enlists the support of the employees to produce the movement.

Learning Goal 3

5.   What are the two attitude profiles developed by Douglas McGregor?
   a.   Transactional and transformational leadership
   b.   Autocratic and authoritarian leadership
   c.   Theory X and Theory Y
   d.   Laissez-faire and charismatic leader

Learning Goal 4

6.   Which of the following is not an assumption about people of Theory X leaders?
   a.   The average human being has an inherent dislike of work and will avoid it if possible.
   b.   The capacity to exercise a relatively high degree of imagination, ingenuity, and creativity in the solution of organizational. problems is widely, not narrowly, distributed in the population
   c.   Because of their dislike of work, most people must be coerced, controlled, directed, or threatened with punishment to get them to put forth adequate effort toward the achievement of organizational objectives.
   d.   The average human being prefers to be directed, wishes to avoid responsibility, has relatively little ambition, and wants security above all.

Learning Goal 5

7.   Which of the following is not one of the basic leadership styles?
   a.   Laissez-faire
   b.   Contingent
   c.   Democratic
   d.   Autocratic

8.   What tool was developed as a result of the Ohio State Studies?
   a.   Managerial Grid
   b.   Least preferred co-worker scale
   c.   Continuum of leader behavior
   d.   Leader Behavior Description Questionnaire

9. All of the following were results of the University of Michigan Studies, except:
    a. To spend less time in supervision.
    b. To give general rather than close supervision to their employees.
    c. To receive general rather than close supervision from their superiors.
    d. To like the amount of authority and responsibility they have in their job.

10. Using the Managerial Grid, which basic style of management has a high concern for people and a high concern for production?
    a. Country Club Management
    b. Authority-Obedience Management
    c. Team Management
    d. Organization-Man Management

11. Charismatic leaders are often credited with the achievement of heroic feats by doing all of the following, except:
    a. Powerfully communicating a compelling vision of the future.
    b. Passionately believing in their vision.
    c. Controlling the behaviors of others.
    d. Putting forth creative "outside the box" ideas.

Learning Goal 6
12. The tough-person, macho culture is characterized by:
    a. the encouragement to take few risks and to expect rapid feedback.
    b. employee focus on how things are done rather than on the outcomes.
    c. big-stake decisions.
    d. individuals who take high risks and get quick feedback on whether their decisions are right or wrong.

13. The work-hard, play-hard culture is defined as:
    a. the encouragement to take few risks and to expect rapid feedback.
    b. employee focus on how things are done rather than on the outcomes.
    c. big-stake decisions.
    d. individuals who take high risks and get quick feedback on whether their decisions are right or wrong.

14. Process culture is:
    a. the encouragement to take few risks and to expect rapid feedback.
    b. employee focus on how things are done rather than on the outcomes.
    c. big-stake decisions.
    d. individuals who take high risks and get quick feedback on whether their decisions are right or wrong.

TRUE-FALSE

Learning Goal 1
1. The use of or desire for power is often viewed negatively in our society because it is linked with concepts of punishment, dominance, and control.

2. Authority is a function of position in the organizational hierarchy.

3. Leadership is the ability to control the behavior of people and make decisions for them.

Learning Goal 2
4. Management is a process of planning, organizing, staffing, motivating, and controlling through the use of formal authority.

5. In practice, effective leadership and effective management will never be the same.

Learning Goal 3
6. Douglas McGregor developed two attitude profiles, or assumptions, about the basic nature of people termed Theory X and Theory Y.

Learning Goal 4

7. Theory Y leaders believe that the average human being has an inherent dislike of work and will avoid it if possible.

8. Theory X leaders feel the average human being prefers to be directed, wishes to avoid responsibility, has relatively little ambition, and wants security above all.

9. Theory X leaders believe under the conditions of modern industrial life, the intellectual potential of the average human being is only partially utilized.

Learning Goal 5

10. According to Ohio State research, leaders scoring high on consideration tend to have more satisfied subordinates than do leaders scoring low on consideration.

11. Country Club Management assumes that efficiency in operations results from properly arranging the conditions at work with minimum interference from other people.

12. Impoverished Management assumes that proper attention to human needs leads to a comfortable organizational atmosphere and workplace.

13. Tannenbaum and Schmidt suggest there are three important factors, or forces, involved in finding the most effective leadership style: forces in the manager, the subordinate, and the situation.

14. In path-goal theory, leader behavior falls into one of the four basic types: role classification, supportive, participative, and autocratic.

15. Transactional leadership involves cultivating employee acceptance of the group mission.

Learning Goal 6

16. Corporate culture is simply "the way we do things around here."

17. The bet-your-company culture requires big-stakes decisions.

18.   Insignificant cultural differences can make it very difficult for an
      acquisition or an expansion to be successful.

ANSWERS

LEARNING THE LANGUAGE

1. Democratic leader	17. Managerial grid
2. Situational leadership theory	18. Leadership
3. Power	19. Task structure
4. Corporate culture	20. Transformational leadership
5. Leader behavior description questionnaire (LBDQ)	21. Contingency approach to leadership
6. Process culture	22. Initiating structure
7. Leader	23. Trait theory
8. Path-goal theory of leadership	24. Work-hard, play-hard culture
9. Position power	25. Entry socialization
10. Culture	26. Autocratic leader
11. Transactional leadership	27. Theory Y
12. Authority	28. Bet-your-company culture
13. Theory X	29. Laissez-faire leader
14. Consideration	30. Tough-person, macho culture
15. Charismatic leadership	31. Leader-member relations
16. Self-fulfilling prophecy	

ASSESSMENT CHECK

1.   Power is viewed negatively in our society because it is often linked to
      the concepts of punishment, dominance, and control. Power can take
      either a positive or negative form. Positive power results when the
      exchange is voluntary and both parties feel good about the exchange.
      Negative power results when the individual is forced to change.

2.   There are three organizational sources of power. These are reward,
      coercive, and legitimate. There are two sources are personal sources
      and these are expert and referent.

3. Leadership and management are not necessarily the same. Effective leadership in organizations creates a vision of the future that considers the legitimate long-term interests of the parties involved in the organization, develops a strategy for moving toward that vision, enlists the support of employees to produce the movement, and motivates employees to implement the strategy. Management is a process of planning, organizing, staffing, motivating, and controlling through the use of formal authority.

4. A person with a Theory X attitude believes the average human being has an inherent dislike of work and will avoid it if possible. Because of their dislike of work, most people must be coerced, controlled, directed, or threatened with punishment to get them to put forth adequate effort toward the achievement of organizational objectives. A Theory X person also believes the average human being prefers to be directed, wishes to avoid responsibility, has relatively little ambition, and wants security above all.

5. A person with a Theory Y attitude believes that the expenditure of physical and mental effort in work is as natural as play or rest. They believe that external control and the threat of punishment are not the only means for bringing about effort toward organizational objectives. Also, commitment to objectives is a function of the rewards associated with their achievement. Theory Y people believe that the average human being learns, under proper conditions, not only to accept but to seek responsibility.

6. A Theory X leader would likely use a much more authoritarian style of leadership than a leader who believes in Theory Y assumptions. A Theory X leader believes that the average human being has an inherent dislike of work and will avoid it if possible. They feel because of their dislike for work, most people must be coerced, controlled, directed, or threatened with punishment to get them to put forth adequate effort toward the achievement of organizational objectives. Theory Y leader believes the expenditures of physical and mental effort in work is as natural as play or rest. This type of leader believes the average human being learns, under proper conditions, not only to accept but to seek responsibility.

7. The leader (manager) would tell the employees what they need to do to obtain the rewards. The leader would also take corrective action only when employees fail to meet performance objectives.

8. The manager-employee relationship is one of mutual encouragement and is characterized by personality on the part of the leader, inspiration by the leader, consideration by the leader of individual needs, and intellectual motivation between the leader and followers.

9. Charismatic leaders powerfully communicate a compelling vision of the future. These leaders are passionate about their vision and believe in it. They relentlessly promote their beliefs with boundless energy and put forward creative "outside the box" ideas. They also inspire extraordinary performances in followers by expressing confidence in followers' abilities to achieve high standards and by building followers' trust, faith, and belief in the leader.

10. The first is substance, the meanings contained in its values, norms, and beliefs. The second is forms, the practices whereby these meanings are expressed, affirmed, and communicated to members.

11. A strong corporate culture is clearly defined, reinforces a common understanding about what is important, and has the support of management and employees. In a weak corporate culture, individuals often act in ways that are inconsistent with the company's way of doing things.

12. The first is the organization has strong values that do not fit into a changing environment. The industry is very competitive and moves with lightning speed. The third reason is that the organization is mediocre or worse. The organizations is about to join the ranks of the very large companies. Lastly, the organization is small but growing rapidly.

CRITICAL THINKING EXERCISES

1. Students answers will vary. The five powers consist of reward, coercive, legitimate, expert, and referent. In a retail setting, referent and reward would best motivate and lead your employees. Referent power is a sign of respect and makes other people want to associate with you. Reward would be useful in a retail setting because most positions would be in sales. Legitimate would obviously be used because of the management title held; however, this doesn't always gain the respect from employees.

2. Your answer will of course be determined by your own experience. The key is to look at how your manager fits into the new style of management, or if he or she is more traditional. If you work for a small firm, it may be that your manager acts in a more traditional manner, for example. But, if the company you work for is a larger organization, management styles may be different.

3. A.   Theory Y
    B.   Theory Y
    C.   Theory X
    D.   Theory Y
    E.   Theory Y
    F.   Theory X

4. As a manager of educated and skilled workers you are less likely to be giving specific instructions to your employees. Instead, you may give them the authority to make decisions, which will allow them to respond quickly to any customer requests. In all likelihood, you will set up a team approach for the plant, using self-managed work teams if possible. Your job will be more that of a coach and team member, allowing for more participation in decision-making and more flexibility for the workers.

    The top manager will be concerned with a broader view of where he wants the company to go. As a first line manager, your job will be more specific, and your goals and objectives more specific than those the top manager has outlined for the entire company. So your directions to subordinates, to the extent you will give them direction, will be more specific.

5.	A.	a.	Autocratic
		b.	Democratic
	B.	a.	Democratic
		b.	Laissez-Faire
	C.	a.	Democratic
		b.	Autocratic

6.	Your boss appears to see the importance of customer service and high quality products in today's competitive marketplace. She has a vision of how she wants the division to operate, which is a characteristic of a good leader. She trusts employees to make their own decisions, thus empowering them with control over their jobs. This helps to create a sense of loyalty and job satisfaction amongst workers. She believes in a democratic leadership approach which is important for effectively managing today's new style of worker. Her leadership style promotes participation throughout the organization. The norms and morals that she has set in place (trust, quality, and customer service) is well-known and expected company-wide.

PRACTICE TEST

MULTIPLE CHOICE

1. B	8. D
2. D	9. A
3. C	10. C
4. A	11. C
5. C	12. D
6. B	13. A
7. B	14. B

TRUE FALSE

1. True	10. True
2. True	11. False
3. False	12. False
4. True	13. True
5. False	14. True
6. True	15. False
7. False	16. True
8. True	17. True
9. False	18. False

Chapter 7 – Organizing Work

After you have read this chapter, you should be able to:

1.   Explain the importance and rationale behind organizing work.
2.   Define division of labor.
3.   Distinguish between power, authority, and responsibility.
4.   Explain the concept of centralization versus decentralization.
5.   Define empowerment.
6.   Identify several reasons why managers are reluctant to delegate authority.

LEARNING THE LANGUAGE

Listed below are important terms found in the chapter. Choose the correct term for each definition and write it in the space provided.

Authority	Organization
Centralization	Organizing
Decentralization	Parity principle
Empowerment	Power
Exception principle	Responsibility
Informal organization	Scalar principle
Job depth	Span of management
Job scope	Unity of command principle

1.   _Job Scope_ refers to the number of different types of operations performed on the job.

2.   When little authority is delegated to lower levels of management, it refers to _Centralization_

3.   _Power_ is the ability to influence, command, or apply force; it is a measure of a person's potential to get others to do what he or she wants them to do, as well as to avoid being forced by others to do what he or she does not want to do.

4. The accountability for the attainment of objectives, the use of resources, and the adherence to organizational policy refers to ~~Responsibility~~

5. The Exception principle states that managers should concentrate on matters that deviate significantly from normal and let subordinates handle routine matters.

6. Job depth refers to the freedom of employees to plan and organize their own work at their own pace, and move around and communicate as desired.

7. A(n) organization _____ is a group of people working together in some concerted or coordinated effort to attain objectives.

8. The Unity of command principle _____ states that an employee should only have one, and only one, immediate manager.

9. The parity principle _____ states that authority and responsibility must coincide.

10. When a great deal of authority is delegated to lower levels of management, it is called Decentralization

11. A(n) informal organization _____ refers to the sum of the personal contacts and interactions and the associated groupings of people working within the formal organization.

12. The scalar principle _____ states that authority in the organization flows through the chain of managers one line at a time, ranging from the highest to the lowest ranks.

13. span of management _____ is the number of subordinates a manager can effectively manage.

14. Authority _____ is the legitimate exercise of power; the right to issue directives and expend resources; related to power but narrower in scope.

15. organization _____ refers to grouping activities, assigning activities, and providing the authority necessary to carry out the activities.

16. _Empowerment_ is the form of decentralization in which subordinates have authority to make decisions.

ASSESSMENT CHECK

Learning Goal 1
Explain the importance and rationale behind organizing work.
1. Describe the elements of an organization.

2. What are the primary reasons for organizing?

Learning Goal 2
Define division of labor.
3. Explain the difference between vertical and horizontal division of labor.

4. List the advantages of horizontal division of labor.

Learning Goal 3
Distinguish between power, authority, and responsibility.
5.   Explain how power and authority relate to each other.

6.   Describe the two theories of authority.

Learning Goal 4
Explain the concept of centralization versus decentralization.
7.   Describe the tapered concept of authority.

8.   Describe today's view on centralization vs. decentralization.

Learning Goal 5
Define empowerment.
9.   List the four elements that must be present for empowerment to exist.

10.   List the actions that can help implement empowerment.

Learning Goal 6
Identify several reasons why managers are reluctant to delegate authority.
11.   Why are managers reluctant to delegate authority?

12.   Name, in order, the steps in the delegation process.

CRITICAL THINKING EXERCISES

Learning Goal 1
1.   You are a manager of the new ABC Fashions retail chain. There are three primary reasons for organizing. Explain how these reasons would play a role in the start-up phases of ABC Fashions.

Learning Goal 2

2.	You are the manager of a computer manufacturing business. Currently, your organizational structure has a vertical division of labor. Do you feel it would be wise to restructure the organization towards a horizontal division of labor? Why or why not? If so, what are the advantages of horizontal division of labor?

Learning Goal 4

3.	As companies are moving away from traditional methods of organizing and taking different perspectives regarding span of control, how can they manage centralization versus decentralization issues?

4.　　You are a manager for Sun-2-Shade, a company that makes a self-darkening windshield for automobiles using the same technology that is used for prescription eyeglasses. Sun-2-Shade is a small company right now, with just a few workers. Eric is the CEO and founder of the company. You are the plant manager. The customers for Sun-2-Shade for right now are automobile manufacturers. Do you think a centralized or decentralized authority structure would be most effective? Why?

Learning Goal 5

5.　　You are the general manager of local Wal-Mart. What would be your stance on employee empowerment? In what situations would you allow true empowerment? Why?

Learning Goal 6

6.   You just received a promotion to general manager position in your
organization. The person whom you are replacing did not delegate
authority. As the new general manager, will you make a change and
delegate authority among lower level managers and employees? Why
or why not? What may be some reasons why the previous manager
may not have delegated authority?

<u>PRACTICE TEST</u>

MULTIPLE CHOICE – Circle the best answer.

Learning Goal 1

1.   Which of the following statements is not true about organizations?
    a.   Most work today is accomplished through organizations.
    b.   An organization provides a vehicle for implementing strategy
        and accomplishing objectives.
    c.   Organizations are a group of people competing against one
        another to gain a competitive advantage.
    d.   Organizational framework consists of both a formal and
        informal element.

2.	All of the following are reasons for organizing work, except:
	a.	to establish lines of authority.
	b.	to improve efficiency and quality of work through synergism.
	c.	to improve communication.
	d.	to prevent theft in the workplace.

Learning Goal 2
3.	Vertical division of labor is:
	a.	based on the establishment of lines of authority.
	b.	based on the specialization of work.
	c.	based on the rotation of tasks.
	d.	based on improved efficiency through repetitive simple tasks.

4.	Which of the following is not an advantage of horizontal division of labor?
	a.	Facilitates the flow of communication.
	b.	Fewer skills are required per person.
	c.	Simultaneous operations are made possible.
	d.	Practice in the same job develops efficiency.

5.	What is the major problem with horizontal division of labor?
	a.	Tasks are too difficult for unskilled workers.
	b.	Tasks are constantly changing.
	c.	Job boredom.
	d.	Tasks are time consuming.

Learning Goal 3
6.	Power is usually derived from:
	a.	seniority.
	b.	presence of mind.
	c.	competition.
	d.	the control of resources.

7.	Which of the following statements on authority is not true?
	a.	Authority is power derived from the rights that come with a position.
	b.	Authority is the ability to influence and command.
	c.	Authority is one source of power for a manager.
	d.	Unclear lines of authority can cause major confusion.

8.   What is the traditional view of authority called?
     a.   Follett's theory of authority
     b.   Acceptance theory of authority
     c.   Formal theory of authority
     d.   Barnard's theory of authority

Learning Goal 4
9.   In the scope of authority, who generally has the most authority in an organization?
     a.   Board of Directors
     b.   Employees
     c.   President
     d.   General Manager

10. Which is an appropriate definition for centralization?
     a.   A great deal of authority is delegated to lower levels of management.
     b.   Allows authority to be spread out equally among all levels of management.
     c.   Little authority is delegated to lower levels of management.
     d.   Full authority is given to the subordinates (employees).

11. What is today's trend in organizations towards the scope of authority?
     a.   Centralization
     b.   Decentralization
     c.   Reverse empowerment
     d.   Absolute authority

Learning Goal 5
12. What is empowerment?
     a.   Promoting employees to management levels.
     b.   Take power away from subordinates.
     c.   Spreading power among all levels of management.
     d.   Giving subordinate's substantial authority to make decisions.

13. Which of the following elements is not required to be present for empowerment to be successful?
    a. Participation
    b. Innovation
    c. Access to information
    d. Independence

14. All of the following actions can help implement empowerment, except:
    a. Whenever possible, restructure organizational units to be smaller, less complex, and less dependent on other units for decision making and action.
    b. Reduce to a minimum the number of simple rules for the organization.
    c. Emphasize a change throughout the organization that focuses on empowerment and personal accountability for delivering results.
    d. Provide the education and training necessary to enable people to respond to opportunities for improvement.

Learning Goal 6
15. All of the following are reasons managers are reluctant to delegate authority, except:
    a. Fear that subordinates will take their job.
    b. Fear that subordinates will fail in doing the task.
    c. Comfort in doing the tasks of the previous job held.
    d. Preconceived ideas about employees.

16. What does the scalar principle state?
    a. States that managers should concentrate on matters that deviate significantly from normal and let subordinates handle routine matters.
    b. States that an employee should have one, and only one, immediate manager.
    c. States that authority in the organization flows through the chain of mangers one line at a time, ranging from the highest to the lowest ranks.
    d. States that authority and responsibility must coincide.

TRUE-FALSE

Learning Goal 1

1. Organizing is basically a process of division of labor accompanied by appropriate delegation of authority.

2. Although called an informal organization, it is formally and consciously designed.

3. Organizing establishes lines of authority that limit chaotic situations.

Learning Goal 2

4. Vertical division of labor is based on specialization of work.

5. Horizontal division of labor facilitates the flow of communication within the organization.

6. Job boredom and humiliation is a major problem with horizontal division of labor.

7. Job scope refers to the number of different types of operations performed on the job.

8. Division of labor is more efficient and desirable in all situations.

Learning Goal 3

9. Responsibility is accountability for the achievement of objectives, the use of resources, and the adherence to organizational policy.

10. The acceptance theory of authority is that people hold authority because they occupy a certain position.

11. The formal theory of authority maintains that a manager's source of authority lies with his or her subordinates.

Learning Goal 4

12. The tapered concept of authority states that the breadth and scope of authority become more limited as one descends the scalar chain.

13. In the scope of authority, the lower level of management determines the shape of the funnel.

14. The trend in today's organizations is toward more centralization.

Learning Goal 5
15. In true empowerment, employees gain confidence in their ability to perform their jobs and influence the organization's performance.

16. In order for empowerment to be successful, there must be three elements present.

17. Self-managed work teams are work units without a frontline manager and empowered to control their own work.

Learning Goal 6
18. The span of management refers to the number of subordinates a manager can effectively manage.

19. Flextime allows workers to choose, within limits, when they start and end their workday.

20. Job sharing is whereby two or more part time employees exchange jobs that were originally assigned to them.

ANSWERS

LEARNING THE LANGUAGE

1. Job scope	9. Parity principle
2. Centralization	10. Decentralization
3. Power	11. Informal organization
4. Responsibility	12. Scalar principle
5. Exception principle	13. Span of management
6. Job depth	14. Authority
7. Organization	15. Organizing
8. Unity of command principle	16. Empowerment

ASSESSMENT CHECK

1. The elements are formal and informal organizations. The framework that defines the boundaries of the formal organization and within which the organization operates is the organization structure. Informal organization refers to the sum of the personal contacts and interactions and the associated groupings of people working within the formal organization.

2. There are several reasons. The first reason for organizing is to establish lines of authority. This helps prevent chaotic situations throughout the organization. Second, organizing improves the efficiency and quality of work through synergism. Synergism occurs when individuals or groups work together to produce a whole greater than the sum of the parts. The final reason for organizing is to improve communication.

3. Vertical division of labor is based on the establishment of lines of authority and defines the levels that make up the vertical organization structure. It also facilitates the flow of communication within the organization. Horizontal division of labor is based on specialization of work. The assumption with horizontal division of labor is that the amount of work produced will increase through increased efficiency and quality.

4. 1) Fewer skills are required per person.
    2) The skills required for selection or training purposes are easier to supply.
    3) Practice in the same job develops proficiency.
    4) Primarily utilizing each worker's best skills promotes efficient use of skills.
    5) Simultaneous operations are made possible.
    6) More conformity in the final product results when each piece is always produced by the same person.

5. Power is usually derived from the control of resources. Authority is power derived from the rights that come with a position and represents the legitimate exercise of power.

6. The traditional view of authority is called the formal theory of authority. With this view, people hold authority because they occupy a certain position. Once removed from that position, they lose their authority as well. The second theory of authority is called the acceptance theory of authority. This theory maintains that a manager's source of authority lies with his or her subordinates because they have the power to either accept or reject the manager's command.

7. The tapered concept of authority states that the breadth and scope of authority become more limited as one descends the scalar chain. The top levels of management establish the shapes of the funnels. The more authority top management chooses to delegate, the less conical the funnel becomes. The less conical the funnel, the more decentralized the organization.

8. The trend in today's organizations is toward more decentralization. Decentralization has the advantage of allowing for more flexibility and quicker action. It also relieves executives from time-consuming detail work. It often results in higher morale by allowing lower levels of management to be actively involved in the decision-making process.

9. 1) Participation
    2) Innovation
    3) Access to information
    4) Accountability

10. 1) Whenever possible, restructure organizational units to be smaller, less complex, and less dependent on other units for decision making and action.
    2) Reduce to a minimum the number of hard rules for the organization.
    3) Emphasize a change throughout the organization that focuses on empowerment and personal accountability for delivering results.
    4) Provide the education and training necessary to enable people to respond to opportunities for improvement.

11.   1) Fear that subordinates will fail in doing the task.
       2) The belief that it is easier to do the task oneself rather than delegate
          it.
       3) Fear that subordinates will look "too good."
       4) Humans' attraction to power.
       5) Comfort in doing the tasks of the previous job held.
       6) Preconceived ideas about employees.
       7) Desire to set the right example.

12.   1) Analyze how you spend your time.
       2) Decide which tasks can be assigned.
       3) Decide who can handle each task.
       4) Delegate the authority.
       5) Create an obligation (responsibility).
       6) Control the delegation.

CRITICAL THINKING EXERCISES

1.   Student answers will vary. Since, ABC Fashions is new, it is
      important to establish the lines of authority throughout the
      organization. This will limit the number of chaotic situations
      experienced in a start-up. Also, utilizing the idea of synergism and its
      effectiveness, ABC can break through any barriers of entry and start
      competing with other retailers. Communication is also a must in any
      organization. Good lines of communication will lead to efficiency
      company-wide.

2.   Student answers will vary. Horizontal division of labor is based on the
      specialization of work. Competing with other companies in the
      industry, such as Dell, it would be a good idea to structure the
      company with horizontal division of labor. This will promote
      efficiency and quality with the same amount of effort. Some of the
      advantages are fewer skills are required per person, and the skills
      required for selection of training purposes are easier to supply. Also,
      practice in the same job develops proficiency. Simultaneous
      operations can take place and more conformity in the final product
      results when each piece is always produced by the same person.

3. Changes in the areas we have been discussing are closely related to the changes we are seeing in the area of decision making. As spans of control widen and non-traditional ways of grouping workers emerge, decision-making is being delegated to lower levels management, or even to non-management levels. Today's rapidly changing markets and differences in consumer tastes are favoring a more decentralized structure, with wider spans of control.

4. Sun-2-Shade is very small with a customer base where most of the needs are similar. In other words, there is no need to customize products to meet different regional needs, only shapes and sizes for different automobile brands. This company could use centralized authority because it is small and decision-making can still be made quickly. Employees probably have easy access to Eric, the founder and CEO of the company, who may want to retain control over his new company for the time being.

5. Student answers will vary. Empowerment can create confidence in the ability to perform. However, managers must make sure that the four elements: participation, innovation, access to information, and accountability must be present for empowerment to be successful. True empowerment allows employees to bend the rules to do whatever they have to do to take care of the customer. Management must be careful about how much bending of the rules goes on.

6. Student answers will vary. Change needs to be able to take place for organizations to grow and succeed. Also, the previous manager may have had a natural resistance to delegating authority. He didn't take risks. It is natural to be reluctant to delegate authority for numerous reasons such as fear that subordinates will fail in doing a task, or the belief that it is easier to do the task oneself rather than delegate it. The previous manager may have had a hunger for power as well. The delegation process should be implemented; however, a gradual change should be put into place.

PRACTICE TEST

MULTIPLE CHOICE

1. C	9. A
2. D	10. C
3. A	11. B
4. A	12. D
5. C	13. D
6. D	14. B
7. B	15. A
8. C	16. C

TRUE FALSE

1. True	11. False
2. False	12. True
3. True	13. False
4. False	14. False
5. False	15. True
6. True	16. False
7. True	17. True
8. False	18. True
9. True	19. True
10. False	20. False

Chapter 8 – Organizing Structure

After you have read this chapter, you should be able to:

1.   Explain the purpose of an organization chart.
2.   Describe factors and changes that affect an organization's structure.
3.   Define a contingency approach.
4.   Identify the different types of departmentalization.
5.   Describe the different types of organizational structure, including a virtual organization.
6.   Discuss the types and effective use of committees.

LEARNING THE LANGUAGE

Listed below are important terms found in the chapter. Choose the correct term for each definition and write it in the space provided.

Board of directors	Line functions
Committee	Line structure
Contingency approach	Matrix structure
Customer departmentalization	Mechanistic systems
Departmentalization	Organic systems
Flat structure	Organization structure
Functional departmentalization	Outsourcing
Geographic departmentalization	Product departmentalization
Horizontal structure	Staff functions
Hybrid departmentalization	Tall structure
Line and staff structure	Virtual organization

1.   The _____ theorizes that different situations and conditions require different management approaches.

2.   _____ are functions that are advisory and supportive in nature; designed to contribute to the efficiency and maintenance of the organization.

3. A(n) _____ is a temporary network of independent companies – suppliers, customers, and even rivals – linked by information technology to share skills, costs, and access to one another's markets.

4. The framework that defines the boundaries of the formal organization within which the organization operates is called the _____.

5. _____ is defining organizational units by territories.

6. An organization structure that results when staff specialists are added to a line organization refers to the _____.

7. _____ is the grouping of jobs into related work units.

8. _____ is an organization with few levels and relatively large spans of management of each level.

9. _____ are functions and activities directly involved in producing and marketing the organization's goods or services.

10. _____ are characterized by less formal job descriptions, greater emphasis on adaptability, more participation and less fixed authority.

11. _____ are functions that contribute directly to company profits.

12. _____ is defining organizational units in terms of the nature of the work.

13. A(n) _____ is an organization with many levels and relatively small spans of management.

14. Defining organizational units in terms of customers served refers to _____.

15. _____ consists of two groups. One group is composed of senior management who are responsible for strategic decisions and policies. The second group is composed of empowered employees working together in different process teams.

16. _____ is grouping all activities necessary to produce and market a product or service under one manager.

17. A hybrid organization structure in which individuals from different functional areas are assigned to work on a specific project or task is called a(n) _____.

18. The _____ is a carefully selected committee that reviews major policy and strategy decisions proposed by top management.

19. _____ occurs when an organization simultaneously uses more than one type of departmentalization.

20. _____ are characterized by a rigid delineation of functional duties, precise job descriptions, fixes authority and responsibility, and a well-developed organizational hierarchy through which information filters up and instructions flow down.

21. A(n) _____ is an organization structure in which a group of people are formally appointed, organized and superimposed on the line, or line and staff structure to consider or decide certain matters.

22. The practice of subcontracting information systems work to an independent outside source is called _____.

ASSESSMENT CHECK

Learning Goal 1
Explain the purpose of an organization chart.
1. List and briefly describe the three stages of organization growth and change.

2. Describe an organizational chart.

Learning Goal 2
Describe factors and changes that affect an organization's structure.
3.   Describe Chandler's study of organizational strategy.

4.   Describe the two systems identified by researchers Burns and Stalker.

5.   What are the potential benefits of outsourcing?

Learning Goal 3
Define a contingency approach.
6.   Describe the contingency approach to organizing.

Learning Goal 4
Identify the different types of departmentalization.
7.   What are the advantages and disadvantages of functional departmentalization?

8.   What are the problems with product departmentalization?

Learning Goal 5
Describe the different types of organizational structure, including a virtual organization.
9.   What are the advantages of the matrix organization?

10.   List the characteristics of a horizontal organization.

11.   Explain the three types of virtual organization.

Learning Goal 6
Discuss the types and effective use of committees.
12.   What are some of the things managers can do to avoid the pitfalls and increase the efficiency of a committee?

13.   Define board of directors and explain the difference between an "inside board" and an "outside board."

CRITICAL THINKING EXERCISES

Learning Goal 1

1. The company you work for is in a transition phase, moving from the craft to the entrepreneurial stage. You've been asked to develop an organizational chart to establish the positions within the company and their relationship to each other. Describe what your organizational chart would look like.

Learning Goal 2

2. You have been a manager at XYZ manufacturing for 20 years. Throughout your time with XYZ, you've witnessed many factors and changes. Outsourcing is one change that has become increasingly common as a result of technology advancements. As a company who now outsources work, describe how outsourcing has changed XYZ's manufacturing.

Learning Goal 3

3.   The contingency approach theorizes that different situations require different management approaches. Describe two situations that would require two different approaches.

Learning Goal 4

4.   You are the manager of a sports retail store, and you are trying to restructure the company to utilize multiple types of departmentalization at the same time. What type of departmentalization is this and what are some of the possible mixes for this organization?

Learning Goal 5

5.   ABC Corp. is a sales company. Currently, ABC Corp. is organized through a traditional line structure. Explain how ABC Corp. could incorporate technology and become a virtual organization.

Learning Goal 6

6.   It is time for the selection of new board of directors for XYZ Manufacturing. What type of skills do you think a board of director should have? Would an inside or outside board be more effective? Explain.

PRACTICE TEST

MULTIPLE CHOICE – Circle the best answer.

Learning Goal 1
1.   An appropriate organization structure:
     a.   helps manage competitors.
     b.   helps prevent behavioral issues among employees.
     c.   eliminates unethical scandals.
     d.   helps foster good performance.

2.   The absence of formal policies, objectives and structure characterizes which organizational growth stage?
     a.   Professional management stage
     b.   Craft or family stage
     c.   Final stage
     d.   Entrepreneurial stage

Learning Goal 2
3.   All of the following are factors affecting organizations in determining which structure may be appropriate, except:
     a.   Political
     b.   Strategy
     c.   Technology
     d.   Size

4.   Organic systems are characterized by:
     a.   a rigid definition of functional duties, precise job descriptions.
     b.   narrow division of work; specialized tasks.
     c.   less formal job descriptions.
     d.   the structure of control, authority and communication in a hierarchical manner.

5. All of the following are benefits of outsourcing, except:
   a. accessing top talent or state-of-the-art technology without actually owning it.
   b. fewer personnel headaches.
   c. guarantee that it will save money or provide higher service standards.
   d. improving resource allocation by allowing growth to take place more quickly.

Learning Goal 3
6. What does the contingency approach theorize?
   a. All situations can be handled with a universal management approach.
   b. Two types of situations: aggressive and conservative.
   c. No one situation is handled identically.
   d. Different situations and conditions require different management approaches.

Learning Goal 4
7. Which of the following is not a type of departmentalization?
   a. Functional
   b. Management
   c. Customer
   d. Hybrid

8. Functional departmentalization occurs when:
   a. all activities needed to produce and market a product or service are under one manager.
   b. organization units are defined by the nature of work.
   c. organizations maintain physically isolated and independent operations or offices.
   d. organizations simultaneously use more than one type of departmentalization.

9. Grouping all activities needed to produce and market a product or service under one manager is the definition of:
   a. customer departmentalization.
   b. hybrid departmentalization.
   c. product departmentalization.
   d. functional departmentalization.

10. What type of departmentalization is most likely to be used in organizations that work around the clock?
    a.   Time departmentalization
    b.   Hybrid departmentalization
    c.   Customer departmentalization
    d.   Functional departmentalization

Learning Goal 5
11. The matrix form of organization is:
    a.   a structure that results when staff specialists are added to a line organization.
    b.   a way of forming project teams within the traditional line and staff organization.
    c.   a form that consists of two core groups.
    d.   a temporary network of companies linked by information technology.

12. Staff functions are:
    a.   directly involved in producing and marketing the organization's goods or services.
    b.   related directly to the attainment of major organizational objectives.
    c.   a group of people who are well-rounded in numerous fields.
    d.   advisory and supportive in nature.

13. All of the following are characteristics of a horizontal structure, except:
    a.   the organization is built around three to five core processes.
    b.   teams manage everything, including themselves.
    c.   customers drive performance.
    d.   customer contact with employees is minimized.

14. Which of the following is not one of the common types of virtual organizations?
    a. A group of skilled individuals form a company by communicating via computer, fax and video conference.
    b. One large company acquires smaller firms that specialize in certain functions.
    c. A group of companies, each specializing in a certain function, partner together.
    d. One large company outsources many of its operations by using modern technology to transmit information to its partner companies.

Learning Goal 6
15. Which method of selecting committees promote a sense of responsibility for all?
    a. Appointment of chairperson and members
    b. Volunteers
    c. Appointment of members who elect chairperson
    d. Appointment of chairperson who chooses members

16. Carefully selected committee that reviews major policy and strategy decisions proposed by top management is called the:
    a. strategic committee
    b. organizational committee
    c. Board of Directors
    d. virtual committee

TRUE-FALSE

Learning Goal 1
1. An appropriate organization structure helps foster good performance.

2. The third stage of organizational growth and change is called the craft or family stage.

3. An organization chart only identifies specific relationships.

4.   An organization structure will not guarantee success, but it will improve the organization's chances for success.

5.   Small organizations tend to be more specialized, less standardized and less centralized.

6.   Organic systems place an emphasis on loyalty to the organization and obedience to superiors.

7.   Outsourcing has resulted from improved communication technology and is having an effect on the structure of many organizations.

8.   The best part about outsourcing is that it almost never requires good management, good contracts or realistic expectations.

Learning Goal 3

9.   The knowledge that there is no one universal method to organize has led to a contingency approach to organizing.

10.   The contingency approach should be viewed as assessing variables and then choosing the most appropriate structure for the situation.

Learning Goal 4

11.   The primary advantage of functional departmentalization is that it allows for generalization within functions.

12.   Product departmentalization is based on division by customers served.

13.   Departmentalization by simple numbers is practiced when the most important ingredient for success is the number of employees.

14.   Hybrid departmentalization is when an organization is continuously changing between types of departmentalization.

Learning Goal 5

15.   The matrix structure is the simplest organization structure and is characterized by vertical links between the different levels of the organization.

16. Staff functions are designed to contribute to the efficiency and maintenance of the organization.

17. A horizontal structure is also called a team structure.

18. Technology plays an indirect role in allowing virtual organizations to form.

Learning Goal 6
19. Committees become more efficient as they grow larger.

20. The Board of Directors is a committee whose involvement varies widely from board to board.

ANSWERS

LEARNING THE LANGUAGE

1. Contingency approach	12. Functional departmentalization
2. Staff functions	13. Tall structure
3. Virtual organization	14. Customer departmentalization
4. Organization structure	15. Horizontal structure
5. Geographic departmentalization	16. Product departmentalization
6. Line structure and staff structure	17. Matrix structure
7. Departmentalization	18. Board of directors
8. Flat structure	19. Hybrid departmentalization
9. Line function	20. Mechanistic system
10. Organic systems	21. Committee
11. Line functions	22. Outsourcing

ASSESSMENT CHECK

1. The three stages, in order, are craft or family stage, entrepreneurial stage, and the professional management stage. The craft or family stage is characterized by the absence of formal policies, objectives and structure. The entrepreneurial stage is when an organization grows first at an increasing and then a decreasing rate. The third stage is the professional management stage. This is when the entrepreneur has been replaced by or has evolved into a professional manager.

2. An organization chart uses a series of boxes connected with one or more lines to graphically represent the organization's structure. Each box represents a position within the organization, and each line indicates the nature of the relationships among different positions.

3. The pattern was based on studies of Du Pont, General Motors, Sears, and the Standard Oil Company. The pattern Chandler described was that of changing strategy followed by administrative problems, leading to decline in performance, revised structure and a subsequent return to economic health.

4. The mechanistic system is characterized by a rigid definition of functional duties, precise job descriptions, fixed authority and responsibility, and a well-developed organizational hierarchy through which information filters up and instructions flow down. Organic systems are characterized by less formal job descriptions, greater emphasis on adaptability, more participation and less fixed authority.

5. One of the potential benefits includes allowing the organization to emphasize its core competencies by not spending time on routine areas that can be outsourced. Also, reducing operating costs by utilizing others who can do the job more efficiently is a potential benefit. Another benefit is accessing top talent and state-of-the-art technology without having to own it. Fewer personnel headaches and improving resource allocation by allowing growth to take place more quickly are other potential benefits.

6.   The contingency approach theorizes that different situations and conditions require different management approaches. This approach, also called a situational approach, was developed because of the knowledge that there is no one best way to organize. It should be viewed as a process of assessing these relevant variables and then choosing the most appropriate structure for the situation.

7.   The primary advantage is that it allows for specialization with functions. It also provides for efficient use of equipment and resources, potential economies of scale and ease of coordination within the function itself. One negative effect is when members of a functional group develop more loyalty to the functional group's goals than to the organization's goals. Conflict may also develop among different departments striving for different goals.

8.   Conflicts will occur if departments become overly competitive, to the detriment of the overall organization. Another potential problem is duplication of facilities and equipment.

9.   A major advantage is that the mix of people and resources can readily be changed as project needs change. Other advantages include the emphasis placed on the project by use of a project team and the relative ease with which project members can move back into the functional organization once the project has ended. Also, employees are constantly challenged, and interdepartmental cooperation develops along with expanded managerial talent due to the multitude of roles the project manager must undertake.

10.
  1) The organization is built around three to five core processes, such as developing new products, with specific performance goals assigned. Each process has an owner or champion.

  2) The hierarchy is flattened to reduce supervision.

  3) Teams manage everything, including themselves. They're held accountable for performance goals.

  4) Customers, not stock appreciation or profitability, drive performance.

5) Team performance, not just the individual, is rewarded. Staffers are encouraged to develop multiple skills and are rewarded for it.

6) Customer contact is maximized with employees.

7) Emphasis is on informing and training all employees. "Don't just spoon-feed information on a 'need to know' basis."

11.   The first type exists when a group of skilled individuals form a company by communicating via computer, phone, fax and videoconference. A second type occurs when a group of companies, each of which specializes in a certain function, such as manufacturing or marketing, partner together. A third type occurs when one large company outsources many of its operations by using modern technology to transmit information to its partner companies so that it can focus on its specialty.

12.   First, the committee's functions must be clearly defined. Those responsible for establishing a committee should carefully communicate the limits of the committee's authority. Also, careful thought should go into the selection of the committee members and chairperson. Size is an important variable because the larger the committee grows, generally the more inefficient it becomes. Members selected should be capable members rather than representative members.

13.   The board of directors is a carefully selected committee that reviews major policy and strategy decisions proposed by top management. An "inside board" is when a majority of the members hold management positions in the organization. An "outside board" is when the majority of the members do not hold or have not held a position with the organization.

CRITICAL THINKING EXERCISES

1. Students' answers will vary. The chart will have a series of boxes connected with one or more lines to graphically represent the organization's structure. The owner of the company should have a box with a line going beneath it to the manager. Each management box should have lines leading to department supervisors and these supervisor boxes would have lines leading to the employees.

2. Student answers will vary. Management has reduced operating costs because we are now utilizing others who can do the job more efficiently. We have also increased our talent pool because we have access to more potential workers without having to directly employ them. XYZ has grown rapidly since outsourcing has taken place because we have allocated our resources more effectively. Also, we have to do plenty of research and bidding on the contracts we issue. XYZ wants to save money by outsourcing without jeopardizing quality or service.

3. Student responses will vary.

4. Student answers will vary. The simultaneous use of more than one type of departmentalization is called hybrid departmentalization. In a sporting goods retail store, sales could utilize functional departmentalization. Product departmentalization could be utilized by separating products into their sport category (such as football products, baseball products, golf products, etc.). Customer departmentalization could be divided into individual customers and team or business customers (local sports teams purchasing large quantities).

5. Student answers will vary. The use of technology allows a company to do many things. First, through communication, ABC Corp. could hire people who work at home to answer phone calls and reply to customer e-mails. Fax machines and e-mails are often used to send out advertisements and information to other geographic locations. ABC Corp. could also partner with another company, such as a marketing company or a new supplier/manufacturer.

6.   Members of the board of directors should have skills relating to the company on which they serve. The members should possess analytical and strategic skills. An inside board is one where the majority of the members hold management positions within the organization. This can lead to a conflict of interest; however, the management has a better understanding of the day-to-day operations. An outside board is one where the majority of the members does not hold or has not held a position within the organization. These members bring in fresh thoughts and ideas, but may not know the company as well.

PRACTICE TEST

MULTIPLE CHOICE

1. D	9. C
2. B	10. A
3. A	11. B
4. C	12. D
5. C	13. D
6. D	14. B
7. B	15. A
8. B	16. C

TRUE FALSE

1. True	11. False
2. False	12. False
3. False	13. True
4. True	14. False
5. False	15. False
6. False	16. True
7. True	17. True
8. False	18. False
9. True	19. False
10. True	20. True

Chapter 9 – Organizing People

After you have read this chapter, you should be able to:

1. Outline the human resource planning process.
2. Define job analysis, job description, job specification and skills inventory.
3. Distinguish between affirmative action and reverse discrimination.
4. Explain formal and informal work groups.
5. Discuss the concept of team building.
6. Define Groupthink.

LEARNING THE LANGUAGE

Listed below are important terms found in the chapter. Choose the correct term for each definition and write it in the space provided.

Affirmative action plan	Job knowledge tests
Age Discrimination in Employment Act	Job specification
Americans with Disabilities Act (ADA) of 1990	Linchpin concept
Aptitude Tests	Polygraph tests
Board (or panel) interview	Proficiency tests
Civil Rights Act of 1991	Psychological tests
Employee leasing companies	Psychomotor tests
Equal employment opportunity	Quality circle
Equal Pay Act of 1963	Recruitment
Family and Medical Leave Act (FMLA)	Rehabilitation Act of 1973
Formal work group	Reverse discrimination
Group cohesiveness	Self-directed work team
Group conformity	Semistructured interview
Group interview	Situational interview
Group norms	Skills inventory
Groupthink	Stress interview

Halo effect	Structured interview
Hawthorne effect	Team building
Human resource forecasting	Temporary help
Human resource planning (HP)	Test reliability
Informal work groups	Test validity
Interest tests	Tests
Job analysis	Title VII of the Civil Rights Act of 1964
Job description	Unstructured interviews

1. _____ the right of all people to work and to advance on the base of merit, ability and potential.

2. The _____ is a written document outlining specific goals and time table for remedying past discriminatory actions.

3. _____ is an act passed in 1969, initially designed to protect individuals aged 40 to 65 from discrimination in hiring, retention and other conditions of employment. Amended in 1978 to include individuals up to age 70. Specifically forbids mandatory retirement at 65 except in certain circumstances.

4. _____ work group established and formally recognized by the organizing function of management.

5. _____ prohibits wage discrimination on the basis of sex.

6. The _____ permits women, persons with disabilities and religious minorities to have a jury trial and sue for punitive damages if they can prove intentional firing or workplace discrimination. Also requires companies to provide evidence that the business practices that led to the discrimination were not discriminatory but related to the performance of the job in question and consistent with business necessity.

7. _____ a dysfunctional syndrome that cohesive groups experience that causes the group to lose its critical evaluative capabilities.

8.   _____ is an act that enables qualified employees to take prolonged unpaid leave for family and health-related reasons without fear of losing their jobs.

9.   _____ states that giving special attention to a group of employees (such as involving them in an experiment) changes their behavior.

10.   _____ are informal rules that a group adopts to regulate and regularize group members' behavior.

11.   _____ is the degree to which the members of the group accept and abide by the norms of the group.

12.   _____ composed of a group of employees (usually from 5 to 15 people) who are members of a single work unit, section or department; the basic purpose is to discuss quality problems and generate ideas that might help improve quality.

13.   _____ occurs when the interviewer allows a single prominent characteristic to dominate judgment of all other traits.

14.   _____ is a process that attempts to determine the future human resource needs of the organization in light of the organization's objectives.

15.   _____ is a process of determining, through observation and study, the pertinent information relating to the nature of a specific job.

16.   _____ consolidates information about the organization's current human resources.

17.   _____ is designed to eliminate employment discrimination related to race, color religion, sex or national origin in organizations that conduct interstate commerce.

18.   _____ is providing preferential treatment for one group (e.g., minority or female) over another group (e.g., white male) rather than equal opportunity.

19. _____ is seeking and attracting a supply of people from which qualified candidates for vacancies can be selected.

20. _____ is the process of "getting the right number of qualified people into the right job at the right time."

21. _____ is a written statement that identifies abilities, skills, traits or attributes necessary for successful performance n a particular job.

22. _____ prohibits discrimination in the hiring of persons with disabilities by federal agencies and federal contactors.

23. _____ are people working for employment agencies and are subcontracted out to businesses at an hourly rate for a period of time specified by the businesses.

24. _____ measure(s) a person's capacity or potential ability to learn.

25. A(n)_____ is an interview conducted using a predetermined outline.

26. A(n)_____ is an interview in which two or more interviewers conduct the interview.

27. _____ measures a person's strength, dexterity and coordination.

28. _____ measures how well the applicant can do a sample of the work that is to be performed.

29. _____ is an interview that uses projective technique to put the prospective employee in action situation that might be encountered on the job.

30. _____ are work groups that result from personal contacts and interactions among people and are not formally recognized by the organization.

31. _____ is an interview where the interviewer prepares the major questions in advance but has the flexibility to use techniques such as probing to help assess the applicant's strength and weaknesses.

32.	_____ is an interview where questions several interviewees together in a group discussion.

33.	_____ is the degree of attraction each member has for the group, or the "stick-togetherness" of the group.

34.	_____ holds that, because managers are members of overlapping groups, they line formal work groups to the total organization.

35.	_____ is a process by which the formal work group develops an awareness of those conditions that keep it from functioning effectively and then requires the group to eliminate those conditions.

36.	_____ are teams in which members are empowered to control the work they do without formal supervision.

37.	_____ is a written statement that identifies the tasks, duties, activities and performance results required by a particular job.

38.	_____ provides a sample of behavior used to draw inferences about the future behavior or performance of an individual.

39.	_____ is the consistency or reproducibility of the results of a test.

40.	_____ records psychical changes in the body as the test subject answers a series of questions; popularly known a lie detector test.

41.	_____ measure the job-related knowledge possessed by a job applicant.

42.	_____ determines how a person's interests compare with the interests of successful people in a specific job.

43.	_____ attempts to measure personality characteristics.

44.	_____ is the extent to which a test predicts a specific criterion.

45.	_____ are interviews conducted without a predetermined checklist of questions.

46. _____ is an interview designed to place the interviewee under pressure.

47. _____ gives individuals with disabilities sharply increased access to services and jobs.

48. _____ provide permanent staff at customer companies, issue the workers' paychecks, take care of personnel matters, ensure compliance with workplace regulations, and provide various employee benefits.

ASSESSMENT CHECK

Learning Goal 1
Outline the human resource planning process.
1. Define human resource planning and describe what it involves.

2. Name and describe the three basic questions/phases addressed by human resource planning.

Learning Goal 2
Define job analysis, job description, job specification and skills inventory.
3. What is the difference between job analysis, job description and job specification?

4.   List the six broad categories of information that may be included in a skills inventory.

Learning Goal 3
Distinguish between affirmative action and reverse discrimination.
5.   What is the difference between affirmative action and reverse discrimination?

6.   What are the Equal Employment Opportunity Commission's (EEOC) suggestions for developing an affirmative action plan?

7.   What are the steps in the selection process?

Learning Goal 4
Explain formal and informal work groups.
8.   What is the difference between formal and informal work groups?

9.   Individual members tend to conform to group norms under what conditions?

Learning Goal 5
Discuss the concept of team building.
10.   Why are teams important?

11.   Describe the linchpin concept and team building.

12.   What are the steps for building productive teams?

Learning Goal 6
Define Groupthink.
13.   What is groupthink and why is it disruptive?

CRITICAL THINKING EXERCISES

Learning Goal 1
1. Sun-2-Shade is a company that makes self-darkening windshields for the automobile industry. The company has just hired Sandra, a new human resources manager. She is responsible for human resource planning. Describe the process Sandra must go through.

Learning Goal 2
2. Sun-2-Shade is a company that makes self-darkening windshields for the automobile industry. The company needs the human resources manager to begin developing job descriptions, to identify the various skills needed to perform the different jobs in the company and to start to develop a recruitment and selection process. Select at least one job that will be a part of Sun-2-Shade's organization, write a job description and job specifications, and develop a plan for recruiting and selecting job candidates.

3.   Do you believe changes in the "make-up" of the workforce – more immigrants, more minorities, more women and so on – have affected corporations from a legal perspective? Explain.

4.   Describe instances when you have been in a formal and an informal work group, using group norms and group behavior in each.

Learning Goal 5

5.　Sun-2-Shade is expanding their workforce and building work teams. As a manager, you are responsible for this process. Describe how you would go about structuring the teams and ensuring their effectiveness.

Learning Goal 6

6.　Describe a situation where you or someone you know have been caught up in a situation of groupthink. What would you do to minimize the impact of groupthink?

PRACTICE TEST

MULTIPLE CHOICE – Circle the best answer.

Learning Goal 1
1.   Staffing activities have traditionally been conducted by:
         a.   line managers.
         b.   financial managers.
         c.   human resource departments.
         d.   production supervisors.

2.   Human resource planning is also referred to as:
         a.   personnel planning.
         b.   competitive planning.
         c.   corporate planning.
         d.   operational planning.

3.   What happens during the transition phase of HRP?
         a.   The organization attempts to answer the question, where do we want to go?
         b.   The organization attempts to answer the question, where are we now?
         c.   The organization seeks and attracts a qualified set of competitors.
         d.   The organization determines how it can obtain the quantity and quality of human resources it needs to meet its objectives.

Learning Goal 2
4.   Job analysis is:
         a.   the process of determining, through observation and study, the relevant information relating to the nature of a specific job.
         b.   a written statement that identifies the tasks, duties, activities and performance results required by a particular job.
         c.   a written statement that identifies the abilities, skills, traits or attributes necessary for successful performance in a particular job.
         d.   consolidated information about the organization's current human resources.

5. Job specification is:
   a. the process of determining, through observation and study, the relevant information relating to the nature of a specific job.
   b. a written statement that identifies the abilities, skills, traits or attributes necessary for successful performance by a particular job.
   c. consolidated information about the organization's current human resources.
   d. a written statement that identifies the tasks, duties, activities and performance results required in a particular job.

6. Which of the following is *not* one of the six broad categories of information that may be included in a skills inventory?
   a. Skills
   b. Capacity of individual
   c. Gender
   d. Company data

Learning Goal 3
7. An affirmative action plan:
   a. involves choosing from those available individuals that most likely to succeed in the job.
   b. is a written document outlining specific goals and timetables for remedying past discriminatory actions.
   c. decreases access to services and jobs for persons with disabilities.
   d. prohibits discrimination based on race.

8. The Equal Pay Act:
   a. prohibits discrimination based on race, sex, color, religion or national origin.
   b. prohibits discrimination against individuals who are 40 years of age or older.
   c. prohibits discrimination against persons with disabilities and requires affirmative action to provide employment opportunity for these individuals.
   d. prohibits sexual-based discrimination in rates of pay for men and women working in the same or similar jobs.

9. Reverse discrimination is:
   a. providing preferential treatment for one group over another group rather than providing equal opportunity.
   b. prohibiting discrimination based on race, sex, color, religion or national origin.
   c. prohibiting hiring of illegal aliens.
   d. increasing access to services and jobs for persons with disabilities.

10. What are psychomotor tests?
    a. Tests that measure a person's capacity or potential ability to learn.
    b. Tests that measure how well the applicant can do a sample of the work that is to be performed.
    c. Tests that measure a person's strength, dexterity, and coordination.
    d. Tests that attempt to measure personality characteristics.

Learning Goal 4
11. All of the following are examples of formal work groups, except:
    a. Command group
    b. Functional group
    c. Task force
    d. Interest group

12. Informal work groups are:
    a. established by management to carry out specific tasks.
    b. formed voluntarily by members of an organization.
    c. established by management to create cohesiveness.
    d. established to create conformity and groupthink.

13. Group norms are:
    a. the degrees of attraction each member has for the group.
    b. informal rules a group adopts to regulate and regularize group members' behavior.
    c. the degrees to which the members of the group accept and abide by the expectations of the group.
    d. formal rules established by the group to oppose group behavior.

14. The Hawthorne effect states that:
    a. giving special attention to a group of employees changes their behavior.
    b. giving rewards to a group of employees is the best motivation.
    c. supervising a group of employees decreases production.
    d. production will decrease when groups receive special attention.

15. Which of the following is not a step in the process of building productive teams?
    a. Encouraging group cohesiveness
    b. Building trust
    c. Encouraging groupthink
    d. Selecting Individuals

Learning Goal 6
16. Groupthink is:
    a. a dysfunctional syndrome that cohesive groups experience that causes the group to lose its critical evaluative capabilities.
    b. a process of generating ideas as a group.
    c. the opinion of the group on each member's individual ideas.
    d. a collaborative effort to formulate strategies for a company.

TRUE-FALSE

Learning Goal 1
1. The goal of staffing is to obtain the best available people for the organization and to develop the skills and abilities of those people.

2. Human resource planning involves matching the supply of people with the openings the organization expects to have for a given time frame.

3. The second basic question of HRP is, where are we now?

Learning Goal 2
4. The end products of a job analysis are a job description and a job specification.

5. Job specifications are rarely conducted by specialists from the human resource department.

6. The skills inventory contains basic information about each employee of the organization, giving a comprehensive picture of the individual.

Learning Goal 3
7. An affirmative action plan refers to the right of all people to work and to advance on the bases of merit, ability and potential.

8. Temporary help are people working for employment agencies and are subcontracted out to businesses at an hourly rate for a period of time specified by the businesses.

9. Title VII and the EEOC require some type of affirmative action plan.

10. There has been a growing number of reverse discrimination lawsuits.

Learning Goal 4
11. Informal work groups have ongoing work and are confined to one issue or product.

12. Informal work groups decrease productivity and lower the morale of other employees and the success of managers.

13. An interest group is an example of an informal work group.

14. Group cohesiveness is the degree to which the members of the group accept and abide by the norms of the group.

15. The more success a group experiences, the more cohesive it becomes.

Learning Goal 5
16. Members of formal work groups often develop a shared sense of values and group loyalty.

17. Success of a group depends on the capability of the members to perform the tasks assigned by management.

18. Groupthink refers to the feeling that the entire group is willing and able to work together in order to successfully achieve its goals.

Learning Goal 6
19. Creativity occurs when group members lose their ability to think as individuals and conform at the expense of their good judgment.

ANSWERS

LEARNING THE LANGUAGE

1. Equal employment opportunity	26. Board (or panel) interview
2. Affirmative action plan	27. Psychomotor test
3. Age of Discrimination in Employment Act	28. Proficiency tests
4. Formal work group	29. Situational interview
5. Equal Pay Act of 1963	30. Informal work groups
6. Civil Rights Act of 1991	31. Semistructured interview
7. Groupthink	32. Group interview
8. Family and Medical Leave Act	33. Group cohesiveness
9. Hawthorne effect	34. Linchpin concept
10. Group norms	35. Team building
11. Group conformity	36. Self-directed work team
12. Quality circle	37. Job description
13. Halo effect	38. Tests
14. Human resource forecasting	39. Test reliability
15. Job analysis	40. Polygraph tests
16. Skill inventory	41. Job knowledge test
17. Title VII of the Civil Rights Act of 1964	42. Interest test
18. Reverse discrimination	43. Psychological tests
19. Recruitment	44. Test validity
20. Human resource planning (HRP)	45. Unstructured interviews
21. Job specification	46. Stress interview
22. Rehabilitation Act of 1973	47. Americans with Disabilities Act
23. Temporary help	48. Employee leasing companies
24. Aptitude test	

ASSESSMENT CHECK

1. Human resource planning (HRP) is also known as personnel planning. It is the process of "getting the right number of qualified people into the right job at the right time." It involves matching the supply of people – internally and externally – with the openings the organization expects to have for a given time frame. It also involves applying the basic planning process to the human resource needs of the organization.

2. The first basic question addressed is, where are we now? HRP frequently answers this question by using job analysis and skills inventories. The second basic question the organization addresses is, where do we want to go? Human resource forecasting is a process that attempts to determine the future human resource needs. The final phase is the transition. The organization determines how it can obtain the quantity and quality of human resources it needs to meet its objectives as reflected by the human resource forecast.

3. Job analysis is the process of determining, through observation and study, the relevant information relating to the nature of a specific job. The end products of a job analysis are a job description and a job specification. A job description is a written statement that identifies the tasks, duties, activities, and performance results required in a particular job. A job specification is a written statement that identifies the abilities, skills, traits, or attributes necessary for successful performance in a particular job.

4. Six broad categories:
   - Skills: education, job experience, training, etc.
   - Special qualifications: memberships in professional groups, special achievements, etc.
   - Salary and job history: present salary, past salary, dates of raises, various jobs held, etc.
   - Company data: benefit plan data, retirement information, seniority, etc.
   - Capacity of individual: scores on tests, health information, etc.

- Special preferences of individual: location or job preferences, etc.

5. An affirmative action plan is a written document outlining specific goals and timetables for remedying past discriminatory actions. Reverse discrimination is providing preferential treatment for one group over another group rather than providing equal opportunity.

6. EEOC Suggestions for developing an affirmative action plan include:
   - The CEO of an organization should issue a written statement describing his or her personal commitment to the plan, legal obligations, and the importance of equal employment opportunity as an organizational goal.
   - A top official of the organization should be given the authority and responsibility to direct and implement the program. In addition, all managers and supervisors within the organization should clearly understand their own responsibilities for carrying out equal employment opportunity.
   - The organization's policy and commitment to the policy should be publicized both internally and externally.
   - Present employment should be surveyed to identify areas of concentration and underutilization and to determine the extent of underutilization.
   - Goals and timetables for achieving goals should be developed to improve utilization of minorities, males and females in each area where underutilization has been identified.
   - The entire employment system should be reviewed to identify and eliminate barriers to equal employment. Areas for review include recruitment, selection, promotion systems, training programs, wage and salary structure, benefits and conditions of employment, layoffs, discharges, disciplinary action, and union contract provisions affecting these areas.
   - An internal audit and reporting system should be established to monitor and evaluate progress in all aspects of the program.
   - Company and community programs that are supportive of equal opportunity should be developed. Programs might include training of supervisors regarding their legal responsibilities and the organization's commitment to equal employment and job and career counseling programs.

7.   The first step is the preliminary screening from the application form, resume, employer records, etc. This step eliminates candidates who are obviously not qualified for the job. The preliminary interview is then used to screen out unsuitable or uninterested applicants who passed the preliminary screening phase. Testing, the third step, is when candidates are tested and compared to standards on job-related measures of intelligence, aptitude, personality, etc. Reference checks are the following step and this is when employer checks past performance based on reports from references. The employment interview is a demonstration of ability or other job-related characteristics. Physical examination is a test shown whether the candidate possesses the physical fitness required for the job. Last is the personal judgment step. This is the intuition and judgment resulting in the selection of a new employee.

8.   Management establishes formal work groups to carry out specific tasks. They may exist for a short or long period of time. A task force, command or functional groups are examples of formal work groups. Informal work groups are formed voluntarily by members of an organization, such as a group of employees who eat lunch together regularly.

9.   Members tend to conform to group norms:
   • When group norms are similar to personal attitudes, beliefs and behavior.
   • When they do not agree with the group's norms but feel pressure to accept them.
   • When the rewards for complying are valued or the sanctions imposed for noncompliance are devalued.

10.   Teams play an important role in helping organizations meet its goals. Groups have more knowledge and information than individuals. Teams also make communicating and solving problems easier. Teams help make organizations more effective and efficient.

11.   The linchpin concept holds that, because managers are members of overlapping groups, they link formal work groups to the total organization. Managers improve communication and ensure that organizational and group goals are met; therefore, managers are, in essence, the linchpins. Building effective formal work groups is called

team building, which is the process of establishing a cohesive group that works together to achieve its goals.

12. The first step in building an effective team is finding and selecting the right people. Group members need to have the right skills and the right personality fit. The second step is to build trust among group members and between the group and management. The third step is to develop a cohesive group that conforms to group norms. Managers can improve group cohesiveness by keeping groups small, giving them clear goals, and rewarding them as a team.

13. Groupthink is a dysfunctional syndrome that cohesive groups experience that causes the group to lose its critical evaluative capabilities. Group think causes members to lose their ability to think as individuals and affects their ability to make logical decisions.

CRITICAL THINKING EXERCISES

1. Human resource planning is the process of getting the right number of qualified people into the right job at the right time. Therefore, Sandra, the new HR manager of Sun-2-Shade, must address the question, where are we now? She needs to determine what positions are needed and if anyone internally is better qualified for the open positions. Next, the question – where do we want go – needs to be answered. Sandra will need to forecast or try to determine the future human resource needs of the company in relation to its objectives. Finally, she needs to take the information gathered and determine how it can obtain the quantity and quality of human resources it needs to meet its objectives.

2. The answer will depend upon what kind of job you have chosen. There are many different jobs that will be a part of Sun-2-Shade: sales, production, marketing, accounting, and clerical, to name a few.

    For a sales job, a job description may be:
    "Sales for a small manufacturing company, calling on automotive manufacturers and/or automotive after market dealers. Sales territory will be primarily based on geographic location. Duties will include sales calls; follow up reports, working directly with production manager, direct input into

marketing program development. Compensation will be salary plus commission.

Skills required include familiarity with electronic communication equipment, teamwork skills, good oral and written communications skills, presentation skills, and a bachelor's degree, preferably in marketing or a related area."

You may make use of any of the recruiting tools listed in the text. Good sources may include current employees, local colleges, a local professional marketing organization, or using an Internet recruiting tool. The selection process should include several interviews, in particular with the people with whom the sales person will work, such as the production manager, or other marketing people, and other members of the team he/she will work with.

3.   As the workforce becomes more culturally diverse, laws protecting minorities from discrimination will be carefully monitored. These areas have become very complex, and a diverse workforce makes enforcement even more complex. However, as more women and minorities with the necessary skills enter the workforce, compliance with these laws may actually become less an issue than in the past.

A major issue has been providing equal opportunity for people with disabilities. Companies are finding that making structural accommodations is less difficult than understanding the difference between the need to be accommodating and the need to be fair to all employees. As the workforce ages, age discrimination may become more of an issue.

4.   Student answers will vary. A formal work group would be one that a manager or professor assigned them to in order to focus on a certain task. An informal work group would be one that they voluntarily joined, such as an intramural sports team. The group behaviors that should be assessed include cohesiveness, conformity and groupthink.

5.   The first thing that should be done is selecting the right people with the right skills and personality fit. The teams should have complimentary skills and get along with each other. Next, it is essential to establish trust among group members and between groups and management. Also, cohesiveness can be influenced by keeping

groups small, rewarding groups rather than individuals, isolating groups from each other, creating clear goals and inspiring group competition.

6.   Student answers will vary.

PRACTICE TEST

MULTIPLE CHOICE

1. C   9. A
2. A   10. C
3. D   11. D
4. A   12. B
5. B   13. B
6. C   14. A
7. B   15. C
8. D   16. A

TRUE FALSE

1. True   11. False
2. True   12. False
3. False   13. True
4. True   14. False
5. False   15. True
6. True   16. False
7. False   17. True
8. True   18. False
9. False   19. False
10. True

Chapter 10 – Motivating People

LEARNING GOALS

After you have read this chapter, you should be able to:

1. Define motivation.
2. Discuss the equity approach to motivation.
3. Explain the hierarchy of needs.
4. Discuss the expectancy approach to motivation.
5. Discuss the motivation-maintenance approach to motivation.
6. Define job satisfaction and organizational morale.

LEARNING THE LANGUAGE

Listed below are important terms found in the chapter. Choose the correct term for each definition and write it in the space provided.

1. Avoidance	13. Job rotation
2. Equity theory	14. Job satisfaction
3. Esteem	15. Motivation
4. Expectancy	16. Motivation-hygiene approach
5. Expectancy approach	17. Organizational morale
6. Extinction	18. Physiological
7. Hierarchy of needs	19. Positive reinforcement
8. Inequity	20. Punishment
9. Inputs	21. Safety
10. Instrumentality	22. Self-actualization
11. Job enlargement	23. Social
12. Job enrichment	24. Valence

1. _SAFETY_ needs are concerned with protection against danger, threat or deprivation.

2. _INSTRUMENTALITY_ is the employee's belief that attaining the desired level of performance will lead to desired rewards.

166

3. _INPUTS_ are what an employee perceives are his or her contributions to the organization.

4. _POSITIVE REINFORCEMENT_ is providing a positive consequence as a result of desirable behavior.

5. _MOTIVATION_ is concerned with what activates human behavior, what directs this behavior toward a particular goal, and how this behavior is sustained.

6. _PUNISHMENT_ is providing a negative consequence as a result of undesirable behavior.

7. _SELF-ACTUALIZATION_ is highest-order need and is concerned with the need of people to reach their full potential in applying their abilities and interests to functioning in their environment.

8. _VALENCE_ is the employee's belief about the value of the rewards.

9. A motivation theory based on the idea that people want to be treated fairly in relationship to others is called _EQUITY THEORY_

10. Upgrading the job by adding motivator factors refers to _JOB ENRICHMENT_

11. _PHYSIOLOGICAL_ needs are needs of the human body that must be satisfied in order to sustain life.

12. _JOB SATISFACTION_ is an individual's general attitude about his or her job.

13. The _HIERARCHY OF NEEDS_ has five levels and is based on the assumption that individuals are motivated to satisfy a number of needs and that money can directly or indirectly satisfy only some of those needs.

14. _SOCIAL_ needs are categorized as needs for love, affection, belonging – all are concerned with establishing one's position relative to others.

15. The _EXPECTANCY APPROACH_ is based on the idea that employee's beliefs about the relationship among effort, performance and outcomes as a result of performance and the value employees place on the outcomes determine their level of motivation.

16. The process in which the trainee goes from one job to another within the organization, generally remaining in each job from six months to a year, refers to __JOB ROTATION__

17. __AVOIDANCE__ is giving a person the opportunity to avoid a negative consequence by exhibiting a desirable behavior.

18. __INEQUITY__ exists when a person perceives his or her job inputs and outcomes to be less than the job inputs and outcomes of another person.

19. __ORGANIZATIONAL MORALE__ is an individual's feeling of being accepted by and belonging to a group of employees through common goals, confidence in the desirability of these goals, and progress toward these goals.

20. __EXTINCTION__ is providing no positive consequences or removing previously provided positive consequences as a result of undesirable behavior.

21. __ESTEEM__ needs influence the development of various kinds of relationships based on adequacy, independence, and the giving and receiving of indications of esteem and acceptance.

22. Giving an employee more of a similar type of operation to perform refers to __INEQUITY__

23. __EXPERTANCY__ is the employee's belief that his or her effort will lead to the desired level of performance.

24. The __MOTIVATION HYGIENE APPROACH__ was developed by Frederick Herzberg and contends that motivation comes from the individual, not from the manager.

ASSESSMENT CHECK

Learning Goal 1
Define motivation.
1.   What are the three common characteristics of motivation?

2.   Explain the sequence used to analyze motivation.

Learning Goal 2
Discuss the equity approach to motivation.
3.   Explain the equity theory and the perceptions that exist.

4.   What actions can be taken to reduce inequity?

Learning Goal 3
Explain the hierarchy of needs.
5.   Name and define the five components of the hierarchy of needs, beginning with the lower-order needs.

6.   In what ways are organizations applying the logic of the needs hierarchy?

Learning Goal 4
Discuss the expectancy approach to motivation.
7.   What are the three basic beliefs of the expectancy approach? Explain each one.

8.   Explain the components of the expectancy approach.

Learning Goal 5
Discuss the motivation-maintenance approach to motivation.
9.   Describe the three needs associated with the achievement-power-affiliation approach.

10. Name the hygiene and motivator factors associated with the motivation-hygiene approach.

Learning Goal 6
Define job satisfaction and organizational morale.
11.   What are the five major components of job satisfaction?

12.   Explain the difference between motivation and satisfaction.

CRITICAL THINKING EXERCISES

Learning Goal 1
1.   Motivation can be analyzed by a sequence of needs, motives and achievement of goals. Think about your needs and the motives that produce actions. What are your needs and motives and how do you plan to achieve your goals?

2.   The equity theory is based on the idea that people want to be treated
      fairly in relationship to others. Think about your current job or a past
      job in which you experienced a situation of inequity. Describe your
      inputs and outcomes compared to the other person.

3.

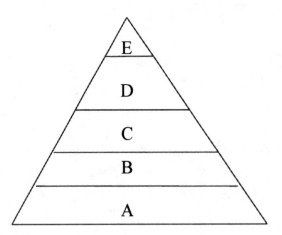

The principal behind Maslow's ideas is that only unmet needs are
motivators, and that needs could be arranged in a hierarchy. Complete the
illustration shown below, and give two examples for each need level, where
appropriate.

        A. _____

            1. _____

2. _____

B. _____

    1. _____
    2. _____

C. _____

    1. _____
    2. _____

D. _____

    1. _____
    2. _____

E. _____

    1. _____
    2. _____

4.   In developed countries, people seek to fill social, self-esteem and self-actualization needs at work. Give two actions that a company or a manager could take to fill each of these higher level needs. What would motivate you?

    a.   Social

    b.   Self-esteem

    c.   Self-actualization

Learning Goal 4
5.   Think about the expectancy theory and how it works for you. Identify
        something you really want. How likely is it that you can reach the
        goal? Will the hard work be worth the effort? For example:
        • What kind of job do you want as a career?
        • What do you need to do to get that kind of job? Is it possible to get
           that job if you exert the effort?
        • What intrinsic and extrinsic benefits will you get from this kind of
           job?

Learning Goal 5
6.   Four job design strategies are:
                job enrichment   job enlargement
                job simplification   job rotation

        Which of the following is being illustrated in each of the following
        examples?

        a.   Employees at Cash Counts, a financial newsletter, are
                combined into a team so that one team has the entire
                responsibility of selling, writing, proofing, editing and
                distributing the newsletter to their own group of clients. While
                each member will specialize in a certain area, each member of
                the team knows enough about all the jobs to get the product out.

                _____

b.   New zone managers at Classic Car Company move from one job to another during their training program, to familiarize themselves with the operations of the district sales office.

_____

c.   At the Mountain City Restaurant, you are an expediter, a host, a busser or a server. The job lines don't cross and are distinct from one another. _____

d.   At the NBC Manufacturing Company, production is such that each worker makes an entire motor, instead of working only on separate parts. _____

Learning Goal 6
7.   Workers at Famously Fresh Industries are among the best paid in the industry. Their factories are clean and workers seem to get along well with one another. "The bosses are okay," one worker is quoted saying, "but they sure do hang around us a lot." The union has made sure that everyone has a secure position. Are these employees satisfied with their job? Explain why or why not using the major components of job satisfaction.

MULTIPLE CHOICE – Circle the best answer.

Learning Goal 1
1.   Which of the following is not one of the characteristics of motivation?
     a.   Motivation is concerned with what activates human behavior.
     b.   Motivation is concerned with what directs this behavior toward a particular goal.
     c.   Motivation is concerned with the results the behavior will bring.
     d.   Motivation is concerned with how this behavior is sustained.

2.   The sequence of motivation includes all of the following components, except:
     a.   Behavior
     b.   Needs
     c.   Drives or motives
     d.   Achievement of goals

Learning Goal 2
3.   According to the equity theory, when workers perceive an inequity, they will:
     a.   try to reestablish an equitable feeling in a number of ways.
     b.   always reduce their efforts in the future.
     c.   always increase their effort in the future.
     d.   generally be mistaken in their perceptions.

4.   Which of the following is *not* one of the questions employees will ask themselves before committing maximum effort toward a task?
     a.   Can I accomplish this task?
     b.   Is the reward worth the effort?
     c.   Will the task include negative feedback?
     d.   If I do accomplish the task, what is the reward?

5. Reinforcement theory is based on the idea that:
    a. attainable goals will lead to high levels of motivation under certain conditions.
    b. perceptions of fairness and how those perceptions affect employees willingness to perform.
    c. the way managers go about motivating people at work depends on their attitudes toward workers.
    d. positive and negative reinforcers motivate a person to behave in a certain way.

Learning Goal 3
6. Which of the following is not included as one of Maslow's needs?
    a. Self-actualization
    b. Physical
    c. Esteem
    d. Social

7. According to Maslow's theory, when a need is satisfied:
    a. the need disappears, and will not re-appear.
    b. another, higher level need emerges and motivates a person to satisfy that need.
    c. it will continue to motivate a person, but not as strongly.
    d. we are content, and will continue to work, but will only be motivated by more money.

8. Harry Leggins has worked for Shavem Industries for a number of years. He has just been passed over for promotion, again, and is considering leaving his employer because it seems that his managers don't appreciate his abilities. The only problem is that he really likes his co-workers, and they have an undefeated softball team. Harry is concerned with satisfying:
    a. esteem needs.
    b. social needs.
    c. self-actualization.
    d. safety needs.

9. The expectancy approach to motivation was developed by:
   a. Frederick Taylor
   b. Abraham Maslow
   c. Victor Vroom
   d. David McClelland

10. According to the expectancy approach, all of the following are basic beliefs, except:
    a. Expectancy
    b. Valence
    c. Instrumentality
    d. Avoidance

11. An employee's belief that attaining the desired level of performance will lead to desired rewards is called:
    a. expectancy.
    b. valence.
    c. instrumentality.
    d. attainment.

Learning Goal 5

12. Herzberg's hygiene factors include:
    a. achievement.
    b. salary.
    c. work itself.
    d. recognition.

13. According to Herzberg, workers felt that good pay and job security:
    a. are the most important motivators for most workers.
    b. were important for participative management.
    c. provided a sense of satisfaction, but did not motivate them.
    d. were the best way to keep jobs interesting and to help them achieve their objectives

14. The strategy of making work interesting and motivating employees by moving them from one job to another is called:
    a. job enlargement.
    b. job simplification.
    c. job rotation.
    d. job enrichment.

15. At the NOVA car manufacturing company, workers are grouped into self-managed teams, which are responsible for completing a significant portion of the automobile. Unlike the typical assembly plant, the car stops along the way, and the team completes their portion of the car before the vehicle moves on. The team is given the freedom to decide who does which job, and they receive constant feedback from the company, NOVA is using a job strategy of:
    a. job rotation.
    b. job enlargement.
    c. job enrichment.
    d. job simplification.

Learning Goal 6

16. Which of the following is *not* one of the major components of job satisfaction?
    a. Attitude toward self
    b. Attitude toward supervision
    c. Monetary benefits
    d. General working conditions

17. An individual's feeling of being accepted by and belonging to a group of employees through common goals, confidence in the desirability of these goals, and progress toward these goals is called:
    a. job enrichment.
    b. acceptance theory.
    c. job satisfaction.
    d. organizational morale.

TRUE-FALSE

Learning Goal 1
1.   Highly motivated employees can bring about substantial increases in performance and substantial decreases in problems.

2.   In motivation, motives produce needs, which lead to accomplishment of goals.

3.   Achievement of a goal satisfies a need and reduces the motive.

Learning Goal 2
4.   The important point in the definition of inequity is it's the person's actual inputs and rewards.

5.   Inputs are what an employee perceives are his or her contributions to the organization.

6.   Expectancy theory suggests that the presence of inequity in a person creates tension in a person that is directly relative to the size of the inequity.

Learning Goal 3
7.   The hierarchy of needs is based on the assumption that individuals are motivated to satisfy a number of needs and that money can directly or indirectly satisfy only some of these needs.

8.   Self-actualization needs are the lowest order needs.

9.   Social needs are satisfied by the development of meaningful personal relations and by acceptance into meaningful groups of individuals.

10.   Compensation systems are designed to satisfy higher-order needs.

Learning Goal 4
11.   The expectancy approach to motivation is based on three needs: need to achieve, need for power, and need for affiliation.

12. Valence refers to the employee's belief about the value of the rewards.

13. External factors are beyond the employee's control and often negatively influence expectancies and instrumentalities.

14. The expectancy that increased performance will lead to desired rewards is almost totally under the control of the individual.

Learning Goal 5
15. The motivation-hygiene approach contends that motivation comes from the manager, not the individual.

16. Both hygiene and motivator factors must be present in order for true motivation to occur.

17. Job enlargement involves upgrading the job by adding motivator factors.

Learning Goal 6
18. An individual's health, age, level of aspiration, social status and political and social activities can all contribute to job satisfaction.

19. Recruitment efforts by employees are generally more successful if employees are satisfied.

20. Satisfaction is largely determined by the value of rewards and their contingency on performance.

ANSWERS

LEARNING THE LANGUAGE

1. Safety	13. Hierarchy of needs
2. Instrumentality	14. Social
3. Inputs	15. Expectancy approach
4. Positive reinforcement	16. Job rotation
5. Motivation	17. Avoidance
6. Punishment	18. Inequity
7. Self-actualization	19. Organizational morale
8. Valence	20. Extinction
9. Equity theory	21. Esteem
10. Job enrichment	22. Job enlargement
11. Physiological	23. Expectancy
12. Job satisfaction	24. Motivation-hygiene approach

ASSESSMENT CHECK

1. First, motivation is concerned with what activates human behavior. Second, motivation is concerned with what directs this behavior toward a particular goal. Third, motivation is concerned with how this behavior is sustained.

2. In motivation, needs produce motives or drives. Then motives lead to the accomplishment of goals. Needs are caused by deficiencies, which can be either physical or psychological. A motive is a stimulus that leads to an action that satisfies the need. Achievement of the goal satisfies the need and reduces the motive.

3. The equity theory is based on the idea that people want to be treated fairly in relationship to others. Inequity exists when a person perceives his or her job inputs and rewards to be less than the job inputs and outcomes of another person. This is a person's perception, not necessarily the actual inputs and rewards. Inputs are what an employee perceives are his or her contributions to the organization.

4. Actions to reduce inequity include:
   - Increase inputs on the job if his or her inputs are low relative to the other person.
   - Reduce inputs if they are high relative to the other person's inputs and to his or her own outcomes.
   - Quit the job.
   - Request a pay increase.

5. Physiological needs are basically the needs of the human body that must be satisfied in order to sustain life. Safety needs are concerned with protection against danger, threat, or deprivation. Social needs are the needs for love, affection, and belonging. Esteem is the fourth level of needs. The esteem needs influence the development of various kinds of relationships based on adequacy, independence, and the giving and receiving of indications of esteem and acceptance. The highest- order need is self-actualization or self-fulfillment. This is the need of people to reach their full potential in applying their abilities and interests to functioning in their environment.

6. Compensation systems are generally designed to satisfy the lower-order needs, physiological and safety. Interesting work and opportunities for advancement are designed to appeal to higher-order needs.

7. The three basic beliefs are expectancy, instrumentality, and valence. Expectancy refers to the employee's belief that his or her effort will lead to the desired level of performance. Instrumentality refers to the employee's belief that achieving the desired level of performance will lead to certain rewards. Valence refers to the employee's belief about the value of the rewards.

8. Each component of the expectancy approach can be affected by the organization's practices and management. The expectancy that increased effort will lead to increased performance can be positively influenced by providing proper selection, training and clear direction to the workforce. The expectancy that increased performance will lead to desired rewards is almost totally under the control of the organization. The final component, the preference for the rewards being offered, is usually taken for granted by the organization.

9.   The need for power states some people are strongly motivated by the need for power. They are likely to be happiest in jobs that give them control over budgets, people and decision making. The need for achievement says other people are strongly motivated by the need for achievement. They are likely to be happiest working in an environment in which they can create something new. The need for affiliation says some people are strongly motivated by the need for affiliation. These people usually enjoy working with other people. They are motivated by the prospect of having people like them.

10.   The hygiene factors include policies and administration, supervision, working conditions, interpersonal relations, personal life, money, status and security. The motivator factors are achievement, recognition, challenging work, increased responsibility, opportunities for advancement and opportunities for personal growth.

11.   The five major components of job satisfaction are attitude toward work group, general working conditions, attitude toward company, monetary benefits, and attitude toward supervision.

12.   Satisfaction and motivation are not identical. Motivation is a drive to perform, whereas satisfaction reflects the individual's attitude or happiness with the situation. Motivation is largely determined by the value of rewards and their contingency on performance. The factors that determine whether an individual is satisfied with the job differ from those that determine whether the individual is motivated. Satisfaction is largely determined by the comfort offered by the environment and the situation.

CRITICAL THINKING EXERCISES

1.   Student answers will vary.

2.   Student answers will vary.

3. A. Physiological
        1. Food
        2. Rest
    B   Safety
        1. Locks on your doors
        2. Job security
    C. Social
        1. Belonging to a club
        2. Family life
    D. Self-Esteem
        1. Winning an award
        2. Getting a desired promotion
    E. Self-actualization
        1. Accomplishing a goal
        2. Getting an "A" in a difficult class

4. Examples:
    a. To fill social needs, companies could sponsor baseball teams, hold picnics or implement self-managed work teams
    b. Esteem needs can be met by recognition programs, recognizing an employee's achievement in a company newsletter, or allowing employees to participate in decision-making.
    c. To help fill self-actualization needs, companies could offer tuition assistance programs, provide job training, allow people to set their own goals, implement self-managed work teams, or provide appropriate rewards for accomplishing objectives.

5. The answer to this question will depend on what your goals are and how hard you are willing to work to reach them. The level of motivation you feel will be determined, according to the expectancy theory, by how strongly you value what you say your goals are, and whether or not you feel like you can "make the grade" or get the kind of job you want. And lastly, in the end, your level of motivation will be determined by whether or not you feel that the effort would actually be worth it.

6. a. Job enrichment
    b. Job rotation
    c. Job simplification
    d. Job enlargement

7.   Workers at Famously Fresh Industries, according to the five major components of job satisfaction, would seem to be satisfied. The relationship among the employees seems to be good, stating they get along well with one another. As for working conditions, it states that the factories are clean, so it can be assumed the workers have good conditions. There is nothing positive or negative stated about the employees' feelings toward the company. According to one worker, the relationship between management is "okay," but it seems that management supervises a little too much.

PRACTICE TEST

MULTIPLE CHOICE

1. C	10. D
2. A	11. C
3. A	12. B
4. C	13. C
5. D	14. C
6. B	15. C
7. B	16. A
8. A	17. D
9. C	

TRUE FALSE

1. True	11. False
2. False	12. True
3. True	13. True
4. False	14. False
5. True	15. False
6. False	16. True
7. True	17. False
8. False	18. True
9. True	19. True
10. False	20. False

Chapter 11: Management Control

LEARNING GOALS

After you have read this chapter, you should be able to:

1. Explain why management controls are necessary.
2. Describe the control pyramid.
3. Differentiate between preliminary, concurrent and postaction controls.
4. List the four basic types of financial ratios.
5. Explain the determinants of performance.
6. Describe the major performance appraisal methods.

LEARNING THE LANGUAGE

Listed below are important terms found in the chapter. Choose the correct term for each definition and write it in the space provided.

Abilities	Leniency
Audits	Management Audits
Behavior or personal control	Multirater assessment or 360-degree feedback
Break-even charts	Output or impersonal control
Budget	Performance
Central Tendency	Performance appraisal
Checklist	Postaction control
Concurrent controls	Preliminary control
Control	Production standards approach
Critical-incident appraisal	Recency
Effort	Role perception
Essay appraisal method	Zero-based budgeting
Graphic rating scale	

1. The direction in which employees believe they should channel their efforts on their jobs is known as ___Role Perception___

2. _[*post action controll*]_____ is designed to detect an existing or a potential problem before it gets out of hand.

3. The _[*production standard approach*]_____ to performance appraisal is most frequently used for employees who are involved in physically producing a product, and is basically a form of objective setting for these employees.

4. _[*zero-based budgeting*]_____ is a form of budgeting in which the manager must build and justify each area of a budget.

5. With the _[*Graphic Rating Scale*]_____ method, the manager assesses an employee on factors such as quantity of work, dependability, job knowledge, attendance, accuracy of work and cooperativeness.

6. The process of ensuring that organizational activities are going according to plan; accomplished by comparing actual performance to predetermined standards of objectives, then taking action to correct any deviations is called _[*Control*]_____

7. _[*Audits*]_____ are methods of control normally involved with financial matters.

8. The process that involves determining and communicating to employees how they are performing their jobs and establishing a plan for improvement is referred to as a(n) _[*Performance appraisal*]_____

9. _[*Performance*]_____ refers to the degree of accomplishment of the tasks that make up an employee's job.

10. Personal characteristics used in performing a job is called _[*Abilities*]_____

11. _[*outputs or impersonal controll*]_____ is based on the measurement of outputs.

12. _[*Leniency*]_____ is the grouping of ratings at the positive end of the scale instead of spreading them throughout the scale.

13. The _[*appraisal method*]_____ requires the manager to describe an employee's performance in written narrative form.

14. Focus on processes as it occurs; designed to detect a problem when it occurs is referred to as _concurrent control_

15. _Management Audits_ attempts to evaluate the overall management practices and policies of the organization.

16. _Central Tendency_ occurs when performance appraisal statistics indicate that most employees are evaluated similarity as doing average or above-average work.

17. The _Multirater Assessment or 360 Feedback_ is a method of performance appraisal that uses input from an employee's managers, peers, customers, suppliers, or colleagues.

18. _Behavior or Personal Control_ is based on direct, personal surveillance.

19. _Recency_ errors occur when performance evaluations are based on work performed most recently, generally work performed one to two months before evaluation.

20. A(n) _checklist_ requires the manager to answer 'yes' or 'no' to a series of questions concerning the employee's behavior.

21. The _critical incident appraisal_ method requires the manager to keep a written record of incidents, as they occur, involving job behaviors that illustrate both satisfactory and unsatisfactory performance of the employee being rated.

22. _Preliminary control_ is a method of exercising control to prevent a problem from occurring.

23. _Effort_ results from being motivated; refers to the amount of energy an employee uses in performing a job.

24. _Break Even charts_ depicts graphically the relationship of volume of operations to profits.

25. Statement of expected results or requirements expressed in financial or numerical terms is called a(n) _budget_.

189

ASSESSMENT CHECK

Learning Goal 1
Explain why management controls are necessary.

1. Controlling is similar to planning. What basic questions does it address?

   Where are we now?

   Where do we want to be?

   How can we get there from here?

2. What can managers do with the information gathered from all forms of management controls?

   Prevent crises,
   stanardize outputs
   Appraise employee's performance.
   Update plans,
   protect organization's Assets.

Learning Goal 2
Describe the control pyramid.

3. What is the purpose of the control pyramid?

   The idea is to implicate simple controls first and then move to more complex controls at a later time.

4. What are the various levels in the control pyramid?

   Fool proof controls
   Automatic controls
   Operation controls
   Supervisory controls
   informational controls

Learning Goal 3
Differentiate between preliminary, concurrent and postaction controls.

5. What are the two categories of control methods?

   Behavior or personal control

   output or interpersonal cotrol

6. What is the purpose of balance sheet budgets?

   Zero base budgeting

Learning Goal 4
List the four basic types of financial ratios.
7. What are the four basic types of financial ratios?

profit ability Ratio
Liquidety
Debt Ratio
Activity Ratio

8. What is the difference between the current ratio and quick ratio?

Learning Goal 5
Explain the determinants of performance.
9. What are the steps required to prepare a report?

Effort ①
Abilities
Role Perceptions
Results

10. What is an advantage of using a balanced scorecard?

It is based on participation and commitment at all levels within the organization.

Learning Goal 6
Describe the major performance appraisal methods.
11. What are the steps in a typical MBO process?

Estabilishing clear and precise defined statements
of objections for the work an employee is good to do.

P-315

12. What are serious weaknesses of the graphic rating scale method?

1. Managers are unlikely to interperet
written descriptions in the same manner,
because of differences, background, Experience,
Personolities, Relationship

CRITICAL THINKING EXERCISES

Learning Goal 1 and 2
1.   Consider the company for which you work or have worked in the past. What value does management controls provide for your organization? In regards to the control pyramid, are controls pushed down the hierarchy? If yes, provide an example.

Learning Goal 3
2.   If you were to become an entrepreneur, how would you control your budget? What is the greatest danger in controlling your budget?

Learning Goal 4

3. Bob is considering investing in XYZ Corporation. What type of financial ratios would you recommend he use in his analysis? Should financial ratios provide Bob with all the information needed to make his decision?

Learning Goal 5

4. Consider the company for which you work or have worked in the past. What types of electronic monitors, if any, are installed to monitor the activities of employees? Do electronic monitoring devices raise or lower the performance of employees?

Learning Goal 6

5. If you were in charge of giving a performance appraisal for employees who are involved in physically producing a product, what appraisal method would you choose? Explain.

PRACTICE TEST

MULTIPLE CHOICE – Circle the best answer.

Learning Goal 1

1.   Management controls can provide managers with information to do all of the following, except:
   a.   Customize outputs
   b.   Update plans
   c.   Protect the organization's assets
   d.   Prevent crises

Learning Goal 2

2.   What is the lowest area of the control pyramid?
   a.   Informational controls
   b.   Operator controls
   c.   Foolproof controls
   d.   Automatic controls

3.   What area of the control pyramid requires a human response?
   a.   Automatic controls
   b.   Foolproof controls
   c.   Supervisory controls
   d.   Operator controls

Learning Goal 3

4.   What type of control is based on direct, personal surveillance?
   a.   Output control
   b.   Behavior control
   c.   Direct control
   d.   Impersonal control

5.   Which of these controls is designed to detect an existing or a potential problem before it gets out of hand?
   a.   Concurrent
   b.   Preliminary
   c.   Postaction
   d.   Prior

6. What type of budget forecasts cash receipts and disbursements?
   a. Cash budget
   b. Balance sheet budget
   c. Capital expenditure budget
   d. Revenue and expense budget

Learning Goal 4
7. Which type of financial ratios is used to judge how well an organization will be able to meet its short-term financial obligations?
   a. Debt
   b. Liquidity
   c. Activity
   d. Profitability

8. Which of the following is a type of profitability ratio?
   a. Asset turnover
   b. Debt to equity
   c. Return on equity
   d. Current ratio

Learning Goal 5
9. _____ is a method of control normally involved with financial matters.
   a. 360 review
   b. Management by objectives
   c. The balanced scorecard
   d. Audits

10. What are personal characteristics used in performing a job?
    a. Abilities
    b. Capacities
    c. Innate capabilities
    d. Talents

Learning Goal 5

11.   The _____ method requires managers to keep a written record of incidents, as they occur, involving job behaviors that illustrate both satisfactory and unsatisfactory performance of the employee being rated.
a.   critical-incident appraisal
b.   checklist
c.   essay approach
d.   production standards

12.   Which of the following is not a commonly used ranking method?
a.   Congruency
b.   Forced distribution
c.   Paired comparison
d.   Alteration

TRUE-FALSE

Learning Goal 1

1.   Controlling simply means knowing what is actually happening in comparison to set standards or objectives and then making any necessary corrections.

Learning Goal 2

2.   Automatic controls deal with repetitive acts and require little thought.

3.   There are five areas of the control pyramid.

Learning Goal 3

4.   Impersonal control is based on the measurement of outputs.

5.   Concurrent control is a method of exercising control to prevent a problem from occurring.

6.   Budgets present no dangers, which explain its usefulness for planning and control.

7.   Under zero-base budgeting, each activity under a manager's discretion is identified, evaluated and ranked by importance.

Learning Goal 4

8. ⊤ Activity ratios evaluate how effectively an organization is managing some of its basic operations.

9. F Inventory turnover and accounts receivable turnover are types of liquidity ratios.

Learning Goal 5

10. ⊤ The activities and behavior employees believe are necessary in the performance of their jobs define their role perceptions.

Learning Goal 6

11. F The primary problem with the production standards approach is that their length and content can vary considerably.

12. F A common error in performance appraisals is the halo effect.

ANSWERS

LEARNING THE LANGUAGE

1. Role perception	14. Concurrent control
2. Postaction control	15. Management audit
3. Production standards approach	16. Central tendency
4. Zero-based budgeting	17. Multirater assessment or 360-degree feedback
5. Graphic rating scale	18. Behavior or personal control
6. Control	19. Recency
7. Audits	20. Checklist
8. Performance appraisal	21. Critical-incident approach
9. Performance	22. Preliminary control
10. Abilities	23. Effort
11. Output or impersonal control	24. Break-even charts
12. Leniency	25. Budget
13. Essay appraisal method	

ASSESSMENT CHECK

1. Controlling addresses these basic questions: Where are we now? Where do we want to be? How can we get there from here?

2. Managers can prevent crises, standardize outputs, appraise employee performance, update plans and protect the organization's assets.

3. The control pyramid provides a model for implementing controls in an organization.

4. The various levels in the control pyramid include the following: foolproof controls, automatic controls, operator controls, supervisory controls and informational controls.

5. The two categories of control methods are behavior control and output control.

6. The purpose of balance sheet budgets is to forecast the status of assets, liabilities and net worth at the end of the budget period.

7. The four basic types of financial ratios include profitability ratios, liquidity ratios, debt ratios and activity ratios.

8. The current ratio shows short-run debt-paying ability, while the quick ratio shows short-term liquidity.

9. The steps required to prepare a report include (1) planning what is to be done, (2) collecting the facts, (3) organizing the facts, (4) interpreting the facts, and (5) writing the report.

10. A significant advantage in using the balanced scorecard is that it is based on participation and commitment at all levels of within an organization.

11. There are several steps in a typical MBO process. First, establish clear and precisely defined statements of objectives for the work an employee is to do. Second, develop an action plan indicating how the objectives are to be achieved. Third, allow the employee to implement the action plan. Fourth, appraise the performance based on objective

achievements. Fifth, take corrective action when necessary. Finally, establish new objectives for the future.

12. One serious weakness of the graphic rating scale method is that managers are unlikely to interpret written descriptions in the same manner because of differences in background, experience, and personality. Another possible problem relates to the choice of rating categories. It's possible to choose categories that have little relationship to job performance or omit categories that have a significant influence on job performance.

CRITICAL THINKING EXERCISES

1. Student answers will vary. Management controls can help an organization prevent crises, standardize outputs, appraise employee performance, update plans, and protect the organization's assets. Decentralized organizations have become more common, therefore students may notice that controls are being pushed down the hierarchy.

2. Student answers will vary. Budgets are the most widely used control device, which can take various shapes, depending on the organization. The greatest danger regarding budgets is its inflexibility. This is especially true for organizations operating in an industry with rapid change and high competition.

3. Bob should focus his analysis on profitability ratios over the other three types of ratios. Although profitability ratios should be the main focus of Bob's analysis, liquidity ratios, debt ratios and activity ratios can provide a more vivid picture of the future profitability of XYZ Corporation. Financial ratios reflect only certain specific information, and therefore should be used in conjunction with other management controls.

4. Student answers will vary. The effects of electronic monitoring devices have mixed effects on the performance of employees. This provides a great basis for debate in class.

5. You should choose to use the production standards approach to performance appraisal for employees who are involved in physically

producing a product and is basically a form of objective setting for these employees. It involves setting a standard or an expected level of output and then comparing each employee's performance to the standard.

PRACTICE TEST

MULTIPLE CHOICE

1. A	7. B
2. C	8. C
3. D	9. D
4. B	10. A
5. C	11. A
6. A	12. B

TRUE FALSE

1. True	7. True
2. False	8. True
3. True	9. False
4. True	10. True
5. False	11. False
6. False	12. True

Chapter 12: Operations Control

LEARNING GOALS

After you have read this chapter, you should be able to:

1. Understand the basic requirements for controlling operating costs.
2. Define quality from the perspective of an operations manager.
3. Explain the concept of Total Quality Management (TQM).
4. Define the following terms: continuous improvement, kaizen, six sigma, lean manufacturing and quality at the source.
5. Explain the purpose of the Malcolm Baldrige Award.
6. Explain the concept of just-in-time (JIT) inventory.

LEARNING THE LANGUAGE

Listed below are important terms found in the chapter. Choose the correct term for each definition and write it in the space provided.

ABC classification system	Malcolm Baldrige Award
Acceptance sampling	Physical inventory
Continuous improvement	Process control chart
Dependent demand items	Process quality control
Economic order quantity (EOQ)	Product quality control
Fixed overhead expense	Quality
Independent demand items	Quality at the source
Inventories	Reengineering
ISO 9000	Safety stocks
ISO 14000	Six sigma
Just-in-time inventory control (JIT)	Variable overhead expense
Kaizen	Zero-defects program
Lean manufacturing	

1. For the operations manager, _QUALITY_ is determined in relation to the specifications or standards set in the design stages – the degree or grade of excellence specified.

201

2. _LEAN MANUFACTURING_ is a systematic approach to identifying and eliminating waste and non-value-added activities.

3. _INVENTORIES_ refer to the quantity of raw materials, in-process goods, or finished goods on hand.

4. Expenses that do not change appreciable with fluctuations in the level of production or service are referred to as _FIXED OVER HEAD EXPENSES_

5. The _ABC CLASSIFICATION SYSTEM_ is the method of managing inventories based on their total value.

6. _PRODUCT QUALITY CONTROL_ relates to inputs or outputs of the system and is used when quality is evaluated with respect to a batch of existing products or services.

7. _ISO 9000_ is a set of quality standards for international business.

8. A statistical method of predicting the quality of a batch or a large group of products by inspecting a sample or group of samples is known as _ACCEPTANCE SAMPLING_

9. _CONTINUOUS IMPROVEMENT_ refers to an ongoing effort to make improvements in every part of the organization relative to all of its products and services.

10. Subassembly or component parts used to make a finished product are known as _DEPENDENT DEMAND ITEMS_

11. _ISO 14000_ is an addition to the ISO 9000 to control the impact of an organization's activities and outputs on the environment.

12. _QUALITY @ THE SOURCE_ refers to the philosophy of making each employee responsible for the quality of his or her own work.

13. Inventory maintained to accommodate unexpected changes in demand and supply and allow for variations in delivery time is referred to as _SAFETY STOCK_

14. Expenses that change in proportion to the level of production or service are called _VARIABLE OVERHEAD EXPENSE_

15. A(n) ___SAFETY STOCK___ increases quality by increasing everyone's impact on quality.

16. Finished goods ready to be shipped out or sold is referred to as ___ZERO-DEFECTS PROGRAM___

17. ___SIX SIGMA___ is both a precise set of statistical tools and a rallying cry for continuous improvement.

18. ___(EOQ) - ECONOMIC ORDER QUANTITY___ is the optimal number of units to order at one time.

19. Counting the number of units of inventory a company holds in stock is referred to as ___PHYSICAL INVENTORY___

20. ___PROCESS QUALITY CONTROL___ concerns monitoring quality while the product or service is being produced.

21. A(n) ___PROCESS CONTROL CHART___ is a time-based graphic display that shows whether a machine or process is producing items that meet pre-established specifications.

22. ___KAIZEN___ means "good change" and refers to a process of continuous and relentless improvement.

23. The inventory control system that schedules materials to arrive and leave as they are needed is known as ___(JIT) - JUST-IN-TIME INVENTORY CONTROL___

24. ___REENGINEERING___ is the search for and implementing radical change in business processes to achieve breakthroughs in costs, speed, productivity, and service.

25. The ___MALCOLM BALDRIGE AWARD___ is a recognition of US companies' achievements in quality.

Learning Goal 1
Understand the basic requirements for controlling operating costs.
1.   What are the types of costs a company can expect to incur?

2.   What is the difference between variable overhead expenses and fixed overhead expenses?

Learning Goal 2
Define quality from the perspective of an operations manager.
3.   What are dimensions of design quality?

4.   What does today's quality management emphasize?

Learning Goal 3
Explain the concept of Total Quality Management (TQM).
5.   What is total quality management (TQM)?

6.   What are the most often cited barriers to adopting TQM?

Learning Goal 4
Define the following terms: continuous improvement, kaizen, six sigma, lean manufacturing and quality at the source.
7.   What is the main idea behind continuous improvement?

8.   How are employees viewed under Kaizen?

Learning Goal 5
Explain the purpose of the Malcolm Baldrige Award.
9.   What does the Malcolm Baldrige Award promote?

10.   The Malcolm Baldrige Award's criteria for performance excellence
       are based upon what seven categories?

Learning Goal 6
Explain the concept of just-in-time (JIT) inventory.

11.   Can the just-in-time (JIT) philosophy only be applied to inventories of raw materials? Explain.

12.   What is the difference between independent demand items and dependent demand items?

CRITICAL THINKING EXERCISES

Learning Goal 1 and 2

1.   Consider the company for which you work or have worked in the past. What are the variable and fixed overhead expenses incurred by the company? How has the quality of your company's goods and services affected the overall company?

Learning Goal 3

2.   If you were a manager of a manufacturing plant, would you
        implement the total quality management philosophy? If you choose to
        implement this philosophy, what activities would you engage in to be
        successful?

Learning Goal 4

3.   Kaizen is a process of continuous and relentless improvement. How
        would you implement the philosophy of Kaizen at Zenith
        Manufacturing Corporation if you were a newly hired manager?
        Explain.

Learning Goal 5

4.   Do you think the Malcolm Baldrige National Quality Award can give
        an organization a competitive advantage? If you were a manager of a
        company, would you focus on attempting to receive this award?
        Explain.

5. Think of a company in which you are familiar with its operations. What inventory control system does it implement? Could a just-in-time inventory control system be used by this company? Why or why not?

PRACTICE TEST

MULTIPLE CHOICE – Circle the best answer.

Learning Goal 1

1. The two aspects of an effective operating system are design and:
   a. implementation.
   b. control.
   c. standardization.
   d. ease of use.

2. What type of cost contains the component of cost of materials that become a tangible part of finished goods and services?
   a. Materials—variable
   b. Direct labor—variable
   c. Production overhead—fixed
   d. Production overhead—variable

Learning Goal 2
3.   What is the primary concern of a product or services specifications in regards to quality?
       a.   Performance
       b.   Appearance
       c.   Reliability
       d.   Can the specifications be achieved?

4.   Which of the following is not a dimension of design quality?
       a.   Performance
       b.   Aesthetics
       c.   Brand
       d.   Serviceability

Learning Goal 3
5.   Which of the following is a popular approach to implementing TQM?
       a.   Raven method
       b.   Carter method
       c.   Deming method
       d.   Smith method

6.   All of the following are barriers to adopting TQM except:
       a.   Commitment to training and failure to install leadership that is change oriented.
       b.   An inability to modify personnel review systems.
       c.   An emphasis on short-term profits.
       d.   A lack of consistency of purpose on the part of management.

Learning Goal 4
7.   Kaizen is a philosophy for improvement that originated in:
       a.   China.
       b.   Japan.
       c.   United States.
       d.   Russia.

8.   What refers to every employee as a quality inspector for his or her own work?
     a.   Six sigma
     b.   Kaizen
     c.   TQM
     d.   Quality at the source

9.   What is a series of voluntary international business standards covering environmental management tools and systems?
     a.   ISO 14000
     b.   ISO 12000
     c.   ISO 9000
     d.   ISO 4000

Learning Goal 5
10. Which of the following is a type of organization eligible for the Malcolm Baldrige National Quality Award?
     a.   Education
     b.   Government
     c.   MNC
     d.   International

Learning Goal 6
11. JIT is also called a _____ because items are produced or ordered only when they are needed by the next stage in the production process.
     a.   demand push system
     b.   demand pull system
     c.   supply push system
     d.   supply pull system

12. The greatest weakness of _____ is the difficulty in accurately determining the actual carrying and ordering costs.
     a.   the safety stock
     b.   ABC classification
     c.   EOQ
     d.   JIT

TRUE-FALSE

Learning Goal 1
1. Fixed overhead expenses change with the level of production or service.

Learning Goal 2
2. The consumer who demands quality may have a different concept from the operations manager who demands quality.

3. Enhancing exhortations for the workforce is one of Deming's 14 points.

Learning Goal 3
4. The Taylor method is a popular approach to implementing TQM.

5. Excessive costs are a barrier to adopting TQM.

Learning Goal 4
6. Six sigma is only a precise set of statistical tools.

7. The essence of lean manufacturing is to look at the entire production or service process to eliminate waste or unnecessary activities wherever possible.

8. Reengineering is a program for making marginal improvements in existing procedures.

9. A successful zero-defects program will have employee goal setting.

Learning Goal 5
10. The most frequently used process control charts are called mean and range charts.

Learning Goal 6
11. Managers do not need to conduct physical inventories because actual inventory is often similar to the level of inventory tracked.

12. The optimal size of the safety stock is determined by the relative costs of an out-of-stock item versus the cost of carrying the additional inventory.

ANSWERS

LEARNING THE LANGUAGE

1. Quality	14. Variable overhead expense
2. Lean manufacturing	15. Zero-defects program
3. Inventories	16. Independent demand items
4. Fixed overhead expenses	17. Six sigma
5. ABC classification system	18. Economic order quantity (EOQ)
6. Product quality control	19. Physical inventory
7. ISO 9000	20. Process quality control
8. Acceptance sampling	21. Process control chart
9. Continuous improvement	22. Kaizen
10. Dependent demand items	23. Just-in-time inventory control (JIT)
11. ISO 14000	24. Reengineering
12. Quality at the source	25. Malcolm Baldrige Award
13. Safety stock	

ASSESSMENT CHECK

1. A company can expect to incur the following costs: direct labor – variable; materials – variable; production overhead – fixed; and production overhead – variable costs.

2. Variable overhead expenses change with the level of production or service, while fixed overhead expenses do not change appreciably with the level of production or service.

3. Dimensions of design quality include performance, features, reliability/durability, serviceability, aesthetics and reputation.

4. Today's quality management emphasizes the prevention of defects and mistakes rather than finding and correcting them.

5. Total quality management (TQM) is a management philosophy that emphasizes managing the entire organization so that it excels in all dimensions of products and services that important to the customer.

6. The most often cited barriers to adopting TQM include (1) a lack of consistency of purpose on the part of management, (2) an emphasis on short-term profits, (3) an inability to modify personnel review systems, (4) mobility of management, (5) lack of commitment to training and failure to install leadership that is change oriented, and (6) excessive costs.

7. The main idea behind continuous improvement is the quality of the processes by which work is accomplished.

8. Under Kaizen, employees are viewed as the organization's most valued assets.

9. The Malcolm Baldrige Award promotes performance excellence as an integral part of organizational management practices, publicizes successful performance strategies, and recognizes the quality and performance achievements of US organizations.

10. The Malcolm Baldrige Award's criteria for performance excellence is based upon the following seven categories: leadership; strategic planning; customer and market focus; measurement, analysis and knowledge management; workforce focus; process management; and results.

11. The just-in-time (JIT) philosophy can be applied to inventories of raw materials, in addition to the production of subassemblies or final products.

12. Independent demand items are finished goods ready to be shipped our or sold, while dependent demand items are typically subassembly or component parts used to make a finished product.

CRITICAL THINKING EXERCISES

1. Answers may vary. Variable overhead expenses change with the level of production or service unlike fixed overhead expenses. The quality of an organization's goods and services can affect (1) a loss of business, (2) liability, (3) costs, and (4) productivity.

2. Answers may vary. As with other management philosophies, TQM has both advantages and disadvantages. If you choose to implement this philosophy, a list of initiatives is listed on page 343 that have led to the successful implementation of TQM.

3. Kaizen is simply a system of taking small steps to improve the workplace. This philosophy can be implemented through teamwork and extensive employee participation.

4. Answers may vary. The Malcolm Baldrige National Quality Award will display the quality of a company's products or services, which can lead to a competitive advantage. While quality is important to every company, focusing on winning this goal may distract management from focusing on its company specific goals.

5. Answers may vary. It is important to note that a just-in-time inventory control system is not appropriate for every company. While this strategy has been effective for Wal-Mart and Dell, this system would not be effective for other companies.

PRACTICE TEST

MULTIPLE CHOICE

1. B	7. B
2. A	8. D
3. D	9. A
4. C	10. A
5. C	11. B
6. A	12. C

TRUE FALSE

1. False	7. True
2. True	8. False
3. False	9. True
4. False	10. True
5. True	11. False
6. False	12. True

Chapter 13 – Contemporary Issues

LEARNING THE LANGUAGE

Listed below are important terms found in the chapter. Choose the correct term for each definition and write it in the space provided.

Absolute advantage	International trade ④
Balance of trade	Law of comparative advantage
Direct feedback	Licensing agreement
Diversification	Multinational corporation (MNC)
Diversity	North American Free Trade Agreement (NAFTA)
Embargo	Organizational development (OD) ③
Environmental changes ②	Quotas
Exports	Sensitivity training
Foreign intermediary	Strategic alliance ①
Free trade area	Tariff ⑤
Glass ceiling	Team building
Imports	Technological changes
Internal changes	

1.   A(n) _____ is when companies pool resources and skills in order to achieve common goals.

2.	_____ are all non-technological changes that occur outside the organization.

3.	_____ is an organization-wide planned effort, managed from the top, to increase organizational performance through planned interventions.

4.	The exchange of goods and services by different countries is called _____.

5.	_____ are government-imposed taxes charged on goods imported into a country.

6.	_____ is a process by which the formal work group develops an awareness of those conditions that keep it from functioning effectively and then requires the group to eliminate those conditions.

7.	_____ are goods and services that are sold abroad.

8.	The _____ allows business in the United States, Mexico, and Canada to sell their products anywhere in North America without facing major trade restrictions.

9.	A method used in OD to make one more aware of oneself and one's impact on others is called _____.

10.	A(n) _____ refers to a level within the managerial hierarchy beyond which very few women and minorities advance.

11.	A(n) _____ is a wholesaler or agent that markets products for companies wanting to do business abroad.

12.	_____ establishes the maximum quantity of a product that can be imported or exported during a given period.

13.	_____ is the ability to produce more of a good than another producer.

14.	_____ is the difference between the value of the good a country exports and the value of the good it imports.

15. _____ are changes in such things as new equipment and new processes.

16. _____ includes people of different genders, races, religions, nationalities, ethnic groups, age groups and physical abilities.

17. A business that maintains a presence in two or more countries, has a considerable portion of its assets invested in and derives a substantial portion of its sales and profits from international activities, considers opportunities throughout the world, and has a worldwide perspective and orientation is called a(n) _____.

18. _____ are goods and services from abroad.

19. A region within which trade restrictions are reduced or eliminated is called a(n) _____.

20. _____ are budget adjustments, policy changes, personnel changes, and the like.

21. Producers should produce the goods they are most efficient at producing and purchase from others the goods they are less efficient at producing is called the _____.

22. _____ is the process in which the change agent communicates the information gathered through diagnosis directly to the affected people.

23. A(n) _____ involves stopping the flow of exports to or imports from a foreign country.

24. A(n) _____ is an agreement that permits one company to sell another company's products abroad in return for a percentage of the company's revenues.

25. _____ is when a company engages in a variety of operations.

Learning Goal 1
Define diversity and explain how it applies to management.
1.   What are the reasons for creating a diverse workforce?

2.   How has the American workplace changed since the 1960s?

Learning Goal 2
Define global management.
3.   What are the reasons countries trade internationally?

4.   What is the difference between absolute advantage and comparative advantage?

Learning Goal 3
Compare and contrast importing and exporting.
5.   How do companies determine if there is sufficient demand for their products/services overseas?

6.   Why import consumer goods?

7.   Explain the balance of trade and a trade surplus/deficit.

Learning Goal 4
Identify protectionism.
8.   What are the different protectionist measures governments impose to help domestic manufacturers compete? Explain each one.

Learning Goal 5
Explain how to manage change and the change process.
9.   What are the three major categories of change (applied to organizations) that can be classified? Explain each.

10.   What are the reasons for resisting change?

Learning Goal 6
Explain the process of organizational development.

11.   What are the phases of organizational development?

12.   What are the five principles for creating a learning organization? Explain each principle.

CRITICAL THINKING EXERCISES

Learning Goal 1
1.   If you were in charge of hiring and staffing, would you rather have a diversified workplace? What are the advantages and disadvantages of diversity?

Learning Goal 2

2.   How does the theory of comparative advantage relate to the development of free trade agreements around the world, such as NAFTA and the EU?

Learning Goal 3

3.   Discuss the issues of the value of the dollar relative to other currencies. What is the impact of a lower value of the dollar? How would American businesses be affected if the dollar was devalued, as the Mexican peso was a few years ago?

Learning Goal 4

4.   Governments have developed a number of ways to protect their domestic industries from what they would consider the potentially negative impact of foreign trade:

        Tariffs   Embargoes

        Quotas   Free trade area

Match the correct type of trade protectionism to each of the following:

_____   a.   The amount of Argentine beef brought into the United States is limited by this form of agreement.

_____   b.   The U.S. has refused to allow the products of Cuba and some other countries to be sold in the U.S. under one of these programs.

_____   c.   Mexico taxes most of its imports to raise money for its government and help their domestic companies compete.

_____   d.   NAFTA is an example of this.

Learning Goal 5

5.   Change forces the introduction of something different about the organization over time. Employees resist change for many reasons. As a manager, explain how you would deal with the resistance to organizational changes?

Learning Goal 6

6. You are a manager for XYZ Corporation. You recognize that organizational performance can and should be improved. Explain how you would implement organizational development.

PRACTICE TEST

MULTIPLE CHOICE – Circle the best answer.

Learning Goal 1

1. All of the following are reasons for creating a diverse workforce, except:
    a. Employee population is increasingly diverse.
    b. Customer population is increasingly diverse.
    c. Increasing diversity maximizes the risk of litigation.
    d. Retaining top talent means recruiting individuals from all backgrounds.

2. In 2050, the projected US non-Hispanic, white population percentage is expected to decrease to:
    a. 68%
    b. 60%
    c. 40%
    d. 53%

Learning Goal 2

3. All of the following are reasons for countries to participate in foreign trade, except:
    a. It is just as easy to start a business overseas as it is in the U.S.
    b. No nation can produce all of the products its people want and need.
    c. Even if a country were self-sufficient, other nations would seek to trade with that country in order to meet the needs of its own people.
    d. Some nations have resources, but not technological know-how; while others have know-how, but lack resources.

4. The idea that countries should produce and sell goods that they produce most effectively and efficiently is known as:
    a. absolute advantage.
    b. comparative advantage.
    c. international marketing.
    d. free trade.

5. Cuba has fertile land, a warm and sunny climate and inexpensive labor. Great Britain has less fertile soil, a colder and rainier climate, and more expensive labor. Given the same combination of inputs, Cuba would produce much more coffee than Great Britain. Cuba has a(n) _____ in the production of coffee.
    a. absolute advantage
    b. licensing agreement
    c. competitive advantage
    d. comparative advantage

Learning Goal 3

6. Selling products to another country is known as:
    a. importing.
    b. trade protectionism.
    c. comparative advantage.
    d. exporting.

7.   When the value of exports from a country exceeds the value of the imports into that country, there is a(n):
     a.   trade deficit.
     b.   balance of payments.
     c.   trade surplus.
     d.   unfavorable balance of trade.

8.   A lower value of the dollar would mean:
     a.   your American dollar is worth more when purchasing a foreign-made good.
     b.   a dollar could be traded for less foreign currency than normal.
     c.   you should trade in your money for gold.
     d.   costs of foreign manufacturing would be the same.

Learning Goal 4
9.   Multinational corporations:
     a.   are corporations with presence in two or more countries.
     b.   are companies that simply export everything they produce.
     c.   do not necessarily have manufacturing capacity in other nations.
     d.   are predominantly small companies that export their products to many different countries.

10. When the Vietnamese government imposes a tax on imported goods, a(n) _____ is being levied.
     a.   embargo
     b.   quota
     c.   boycott
     d.   tariff

11. A total ban on the import of a good from a particular country is called a(n):
     a.   tariff.
     b.   embargo.
     c.   licensing agreement.
     d.   quota.

12. A wholesaler or agent who markets products for companies wanting to do business abroad is called a:
    a.   licensing agent.
    b.   marketing agent.
    c.   foreign intermediary.
    d.   wholesaling agent.

Learning Goal 5
13. Which of the following is not a category of change?
    a.   Environmental
    b.   Internal
    c.   Technological
    d.   Implied

14. Which of the following is not a reason for resisting change?
    a.   Fear of the unknown
    b.   Additional work and inconvenience
    c.   Fear that skills and expertise will gain value
    d.   Economics

Learning Goal 6
15. The process in which the change agent communicates the information gathered through diagnosis directly to the affected people is called:
    a.   direct feedback.
    b.   team building.
    c.   evaluation.
    d.   sensitivity training.

TRUE-FALSE

Learning Goal 1
1.   In the 1960s and 1970s, women in the workforce filled primarily service and support roles (i.e. secretaries, waitresses).

2.   The trend toward greater diversity is expected to continue over the next 50 years.

3.   Greater diversity only allows organizations to respond to a diverse group of employees.

Learning Goal 2

4.   Absolute advantage states that producers should produce goods they are most efficient at producing.

5.   Most of the world today depends on international trade to maintain its standard of living.

Learning Goal 3

6.   The U.S. is the largest exporter in the world.

7.   About 50 percent of the world's consumers live inside the United States.

8.   Imports are goods and services purchased from abroad.

9.   A country that imports more than it exports runs a trade deficit.

10.   Exchange rates can be quoted in dollars per unit of foreign currency or units of foreign currency per dollar.

Learning Goal 4

11.   A tariff is a restriction on the quantity of a good that can enter a country.

12.   The largest free trade area in the world is in Europe.

13.   A multinational corporation is a business that maintains a presence in two or more countries, has a considerable portion of its assets invested in and derives a substantial portion of its sales and profits from international activities, considers opportunities throughout the world, and has a worldwide perspective and orientation.

Learning Goal 5

14.   Both technological and environmental changes occur outside an organization and can create the need for internal change.

15.   *Presenting* a new alternative is Lewin's first step to successfully implementing change.

Learning Goal 6

16. Organizational development seeks to change attitudes, values, and management practices in an effort to improve organizational performance.

17. An organizational development effort starts with the implementation of a change towards improvement.

18. Sensitivity training is designed to make one more aware of oneself and one's impact on others.

ANSWERS

LEARNING THE LANGUAGE

1. Strategic alliance	14. Balance of trade
2. Environmental changes	15. Technological changes
3. Organizational development	16. Diversity
4. International trade	17. Multinational Corporation
5. Tariff	18. Imports
6. Team building	19. Free trade area
7. Exports	20. Internal changes
8. North American Free Trade Agreement (NAFTA)	21. Law of comparative advantage
9. Sensitivity training	22. Direct feedback
10. Glass ceiling	23. Embargo
11. Foreign intermediary	24. Licensing agreement
12. Quotas	25. Diversification
13. Absolute advantage	

ASSESSMENT CHECK

1. Reasons for creating a diverse workforce:
   - Employee population is increasingly diverse.
   - Customer population is increasingly diverse.
   - Retaining top talent means recruiting individuals from all backgrounds.
   - Increasing diversity minimizes the risk of litigation.

2.	Business was dominated by white males in the United States until the 1970s. For the most part, managers managed people who came from backgrounds that were similar to their own. By the year 2006, most workplaces included women and minorities. Increasing diversity has helped companies understand the needs of their increasingly diverse customer bases. Minorities are expected to make up almost half of the population by the middle of the twenty-first century and the future workplace is expected to become even more diverse than today.

3.	First, a country may not be able to produce a good it wants. Countries may also trade because they have an advantage over other countries in producing particular goods or services.

4.	Different countries are endowed with different resources. An absolute advantage is the ability to produce more of a good than another producer with the same quantity of inputs. Countries need not have an absolute advantage in the production of a good to trade. The law of comparative advantage states that producers should produce the goods they are most efficient at producing and purchase from others the goods they are less efficient at producing.

5.	Companies analyze demographic figures, economic data, country reports, consumer tastes, and competition in the markets they are considering. Managers contact the International Trade Administration of the U.S. Department of Commerce, foreign consulates and embassies, and foreign and international trade organizations. They will also visit the countries they are considering and conduct surveys.

6.	Companies import products that they can resell in their own country. They import these goods because consumers want to purchase them. Some of these goods are less expensive than domestically manufactured products, and others are simply popular.

7.	The balance of trade is the difference between the value of the goods a country exports and the value of the goods it imports. A country that exports more than it imports runs a trade surplus. A country that imports more than it exports runs a trade deficit.

8. Governments will impose protectionist measures such as tariffs, quotas, embargoes and free trade areas. A tariff is a tax on imports. The purpose is to raise the price of foreign goods in order to allow domestic manufacturers to compete. Quotas are restrictions on the quantity of a good that can enter a country. An embargo is a total ban on the import of a good from a particular country. A free trade area is a region within which trade restrictions are reduced or eliminated. These areas are created to promote international trade and limit protectionism.

9. The three major categories are technological, environmental, and internal to the organization. Technological changes include such things as new equipment and new processes. Environmental changes are all the non-technological changes that occur outside the organization. Internal changes include such things as budget adjustments and personnel changes.

10. Reasons for resisting change:
   - Fear of the unknown
   - Economics
   - Fear that skills and expertise will lose value
   - Threats to power
   - Additional work and inconvenience
   - Threats to interpersonal relations

11. The phases of organizational development are, in order: diagnosis, change planning, intervention/education and evaluation.

12. Principles for creating a learning environment:
   - Systems thinking: Managers must learn to see the big picture and not concentrate only on their part; they must learn to recognize the effects of one level of learning on another.
   - Personal mastery: Individual managers and employees must be empowered to experiment, innovate, and explore.
   - Mental models: Managers and employees should be encouraged to develop mental models as ways of stretching their minds to find new and better ways of doing things.

- Shared vision: Managers should develop and communicate a shared vision that can be used as a framework for addressing problems and opportunities.
- Team learning: Team learning is the process of aligning a team so as to avoid wasted energy and to get the desired results.

CRITICAL THINKING EXERCISES

1. Diversity includes people of different genders, races, religions, nationalities, ethnic groups, age groups and physical abilities. This allows for a wide range of views and improved decision making. The advantages of diversity are improved response toward a diverse group of employees and customers. Diversity also helps globalization. Diversity helps to create an organization culture that is more tolerant of different behavioral styles and wider views. Challenges will arise with diversity. New human resource policies must be created to respond to the needs of the individual employees. Communication problems will also arise. However, the result of diversity will be greater than the challenges that face the organizations

2. The theory of comparative advantage states that a country should sell to other countries those products that it produces most effectively and efficiently, and buy from other countries those products that it cannot produce as effectively or efficiently. The development of free trade agreements such as NAFTA and the EU can enable trading partners not only to reduce prices of traded products within those countries, but to also use comparative advantage to their benefit to realize mutually beneficial exchanges for all members, by focusing their efforts on those products and services on which each member has a comparative advantage. The trading blocs have an economic advantage that can make them a strong competitor in the global market, better able to take advantage of the theory of comparative advantage.

3. A lower value of the dollar means that a dollar is traded for less foreign currency than normal. Foreign goods would become more expensive because it would take more dollars to buy them. It also makes American goods cheaper to foreign buyers because it would take less foreign currency to buy them. In the long run, this could benefit U.S. firms in foreign markets. Devaluing a currency means lowering the value of a nation's currency relative to other currencies.

This can cause problems with changes in labor cost, material costs, and financing.

American businesses would find their products less expensive in foreign countries, which could be beneficial for sales, but their cost of doing business in foreign countries could be negatively affected by devaluation.

4. a. Quotas
    b. Embargoes
    c. Tariffs
    d. Free trade area

5. Student answers will vary. Prior to implementing a change, present the idea to the employees to see their perception or reaction. Try to help them foresee how the change will affect them in a positive manner. Also, as a manager, you must establish trust with your employees. If they have confidence in management, they are much more likely to accept change. When a change is being implemented, involve the employees. Also, make sure that any proposed changes are reasonable. Never attempt to force change through the use of threats. When implementing the change, try to follow a sensible time schedule. A gradual change is easier to accept than a sudden one.

6. After recognizing that performance needs improvement, management must begin gathering and analyzing information. A plan for analyzing the data should be developed even before the data are collected. Data can be gotten from any available records or documents that may be pertinent. Employees can be asked to fill out surveys and management may issue personal interviews with the employees. Management can also gather information through direct observation. The data collected must be interpreted to determine the best plan for improvement. Management needs to identify specific problem areas and outline the steps for resolving the problems. Then, the information should be shared with the employees that are affected and help them to realize the need for change. The final phase of organizational development is to evaluate the results. Did the OD process produce the desired results?

PRACTICE TEST

MULTIPLE CHOICE			TRUE FALSE	

MULTIPLE CHOICE

1. C	9. A
2. D	10. D
3. A	11. B
4. B	12. C
5. A	13. D
6. D	14. C
7. C	15. A
8. B	

TRUE FALSE

1. True	11. False
2. True	12. False
3. False	13. True
4. False	14. True
5. True	15. False
6. True	16. True
7. False	17. False
8. True	18. True
9. True	
10. True	

Chapter 14 – Management in the 21st Century

LEARNING GOALS

After you have read this chapter, you should be able to:

1. Discuss how managers might manage in the future.
2. Identify how technology impacts the managerial role.
3. Review the challenges of managing a virtual team.
4. Discuss social responsibility and organization's code of ethics.
5. Identify laws pertaining to ethics in business.
6. Explain social responsibility.

LEARNING THE LANGUAGE

Listed below are important terms found in the chapter. Choose the correct term for each definition and write it in the space provided.

Code of ethics	Social responsibility
Ethics	Stakeholders
Intellectual property	Virtual organization
Social audit	

1. _____ refers to a set of moral principles or values that govern behavior.

2. _____ is ownership of ideas; it gives creators the exclusive right to market and sell their work.

3. A(n) _____ is a method used by management to evaluate the success or lack of success of programs designed to improve the social performance of the organization.

4. A(n) _____ is a temporary network of independent companies – suppliers, customers and even rivals – linked by information technology to share skills, costs and access to one another's markets.

5. _____ is the obligation that individuals or businesses have to help solve social problems.

6. A document that outlines the principles of conduct to be used in making decisions within an organization is called a(n) _____.

7. _____ are the people – employees, customers, suppliers, and the community – affected by the actions of a business.

ASSESSMENT CHECK

Learning Goal 1
Discuss how managers might manage in the future.
1. What were the projections about organizations and management that the authors of the book *Beyond Workplace 2000* made?

Learning Goal 2
Identify how technology impacts the managerial role.
2. How has technology condensed the time and space in the life of a manager?

3. What is ERP and what does it have to offer?

Review the challenges of managing a virtual team.
4.	What are the challenges faced with virtual management?

5.	What are the three common types of virtual organizations?

Discuss social responsibility and organization's code of ethics.
6.	What are some of the areas covered in a code of ethics?

7.	When dealing with an ethical dilemma, what series of questions should you ask yourself?

Identify laws pertaining to ethics in business.
8.   What regulations have been created since the late nineteenth century to make sure that companies do not engage in anticompetitive behavior? Explain each one.

9.   What laws have been implemented to protect consumers in the U.S. against unethical and unsafe business practices? Explain each one.

Learning Goal 6
Explain social responsibility.
10.   Views toward social responsibility evolved through what three schools of thought? Explain each one.

11.   What are the steps involved in conducting a social audit?

CRITICAL THINKING EXERCISES

Learning Goal 1

1.   Read the projections that the authors of the book *Beyond Workplace 2000* made pertaining to organizations and management in the twenty-first century. Do you agree? How do you see it different? What are your predictions for organizations and management of the 21st century?

Learning Goal 2

2.   Choose a well-known corporation (i.e. Wal-Mart, Dell, Apple, etc.) and describe how technology has affected the business over the last 50 years.

Learning Goal 3

3.　You are the manager of a large corporation. You need extra customer service representatives for the Christmas season. You decide to try hiring temporary employees who work at home and have their own computers. Describe some of the challenges you will face with this new type of virtual organization.

Learning Goal 4

4.　You are the buyer for a major manufacturer of automotive parts and have control over multi-million dollar contracts. You were recently talking with one of your suppliers and mentioned that you were planning a pleasure trip to Los Angeles with your family, and weren't sure yet where you would be staying. "It's so expensive in L.A. I'm afraid we won't find a decent place to stay," you said. The supplier said that he has contacts in L.A. in the hotel industry, and that he would not only make the reservation for you, but would pay for the hotel stay for you and your family.

Your company's policy regarding "gifts" from suppliers is not entirely clear. Tangible gifts with a value over $50 are not to be accepted. Other things such as dinners and other intangibles are to be evaluated on a case-by-case basis, and acceptance is left up to the discretion of the employee. Any employee who violates the policy could face severe penalties, including dismissal.

Is this an ethical dilemma? Why or why not? What ethical issues are involved? Is there a question of "legal versus ethical"? What would you do?

Learning Goal 6

5.   Social responsibility is the obligation that individuals or businesses have the help to solve social problems. Read the situation described below and answer the questions that follow:

MUMC is a successful medium-sized firm that supplies parts for electric motors. Dan Furlong, the president, was being interviewed by the business features writer of the local newspaper. The reporter asked Dan his views on social responsibility and how MUMC reflected a socially responsive position. Dan replied although he had never done a so-called social audit, he believed that the firm was a good corporate citizen. He said, "We pay our employees a good salary, and the guys in the shop are getting paid above wages for this area. We make a profit, and give everyone a bonus at the holidays. We take a lot of precautions in the shop, and no one has had an accident to speak of in several years. A few cuts or bruises, but that's part of that kind of job. Whenever we have customer complaints, I make sure someone handles them right away. We charge what I think is a fair price for our product, which I think is higher quality than most of my competitors. I pay my bills on time and don't cheat on my taxes. I guess you could say that we are a pretty socially responsible company."

a.   In keeping with the idea of social audits and socially responsible business activities, is Mr. Furlong running the business in a socially responsible manner?

b.   Who are Mr. Furlong's stakeholders?

     c.   What suggestions can you make to improve MUMC's social responsibility position?

PRACTICE TEST

MULTIPLE CHOICE – Circle the best answer.

Learning Goal 1
1.   Which of the following is not one of the key areas that will dominate the future of management?
    a.   Continued rise in virtual management
    b.   Growth in technology
    c.   Increased focus on competitive advantages
    d.   Increased focus on ethical and social responsibilities

Learning Goal 2
2.   Amazon.com is an example of:
    a.   a click-and-mortar online vendor.
    b.   a brick-and-mortar store.
    c.   B2B.
    d.   a retail outlet.

3. The interconnection of all the functional departments of an organization on one common framework is called:
   a. a Virtual organization.
   b. CRM, Customer relationship management.
   c. Moore's Law.
   d. ERP, Enterprise resource planning.

4. CRM promises:
   a. organizations can track every interaction with their customers and for customers to know the whereabouts of their order.
   b. to give everyone in the organization instant access to the information they need to make key decisions.
   c. improved efficiency through the deliberate elimination of waste and rework.
   d. custom ordering of products.

Learning Goal 3
5. Which of the following is not one of the challenges faced by managers of virtual organizations?
   a. How do you manage a team that may be spread across 50 states or 20 countries?
   b. Is outsourcing and virtual employees really going to lower labor costs?
   c. How do you build a team when the team members never meet in person?
   d. How do you know you can maintain quality while working though a third-party vendor?

6. All of the following are benefits of virtual organizations, except:
   a. Decreases cost of doing business
   b. Improves the work environment
   c. Provides competitive advantage
   d. Requires staff reeducation

7.   Which of the following is not an area typically covered in a code of ethics?
     a.   Honesty
     b.   Security
     c.   Dividend payments
     d.   Employment practices

8.   Sometimes an obvious choice from an ethical standpoint has personal or professional drawbacks. An example might be when a supervisor asks you to do something unethical, and you face negative consequences if you refuse. When you are in such a situation you are faced with:
     a.   two lousy choices.
     b.   an ethical dilemma.
     c.   deciding the legality of your choice.
     d.   a social responsibility issue.

9.   All of the following are questions to help in solving an ethical dilemma, except:
     a.   Have you defined the problem accurately?
     b.   Could you disclose without qualm your decision or action to your boss, your CEO, the BoD, your family, and society as a whole?
     c.   How will this benefit me?
     d.   How would you define the problem if you stood on the other side of the fence?

Learning Goal 5

10. What legislative act makes it illegal to charge different prices to different wholesale customers?
     a.   Clayton Act of 1914
     b.   Wheeler-Lea Act of 1938
     c.   Sherman Act of 1890
     d.   Sarbanes-Oxley Act

11. Which of the following laws gives the EPA the authority to set standards on the type and quantity of pollutants that industries can put into bodies of water?
    a. The Clean Air Act of 1970
    b. The Toxic Substances Control Act of 1976
    c. The National Environmental Policy Act of 1969
    d. The Clean Water Act of 1977

12. Intellectual property rights are guaranteed through all of the following except:
    a. Patents
    b. Copyright laws
    c. Design of product
    d. Trademarks

Learning Goal 6
13. Views toward social responsibility evolved through three distinct schools of thought. Which of the follow is *not* one of those schools of thought?
    a. Profit maximization
    b. Stakeholder management
    c. Social Involvement
    d. Trusteeship management

14. All of the following are steps for accomplishing a social audit, except:
    a. Examine shareholder expectations and dividend policy.
    b. Monitor accomplishments or progress in each program area.
    c. Examine and then set social objectives and meaningful priorities.
    d. Plan and implement strategies and objectives in each program area.

TRUE-FALSE

Learning Goal 1
1. Three key areas will dominate the future of management: the growth of technology, the continued rise in virtual management, and the increased focus on ethical and social responsibilities.

Learning Goal 2

2. Amazon.com is an example of consumer-to-consumer.

3. Enterprise resource planning promised the capacity for tracking every interaction with their customers.

Learning Goal 3

4. A virtual organization is a temporary network of independent companies linked by information technology to share skills, costs and access to one another's markets.

5. Virtual organizations are fluid, flexible and constantly changing.

6. Many people believe that virtual organizations are just a phase.

Learning Goal 4

7. A code of ethics is a document that outlines the principles of conduct to be used in making decisions within an organization.

8. Establishing a code of ethics eliminates unethical behavior.

9. Ethical dilemmas are situations in which the ethical course of action is not clear.

Learning Goal 5

10. The Wheeler-Lea Act of 1938 makes it illegal for companies to monopolize trade.

11. The National Environmental Policy Act of 1969 is the comprehensive federal law that regulates air emissions.

12. Intellectual property refers to ownership of ideas, such as inventions, books, movies and computer programs.

Learning Goal 6

13. A company can demonstrate its sense of social responsibility by contributing its money or time to charitable, cultural and civic organizations.

14. A social audit allows management to evaluate the success or lack of success of programs designed to improve the social performance of the organization.

ANSWERS

LEARNING THE LANGUAGE

1. Ethics	5. Social responsibility
2. Intellectual property	6. Code of ethics
3. Social audit	7. Stakeholders
4. Virtual organization	

ASSESSMENT CHECK

1. Projections:
   - Most American companies will find that they no longer can gain a competitive advantage from further improvements in quality, service, cost or speed, since the gap between rivals on these traditional measures of performance will all but close.
   - Every American business and every employee who works for an American business will be forced to become agile, flexible and highly adaptive, since the product or service they will provide and the business processes they will employ will be in a constant state of change.
   - Every American company will be forced to develop a much better understanding of what it does truly well and will invest its limited resources in developing and sustaining superiority in that unique knowledge, skill or capability.
   - Organizational structures will become extremely fluid. No longer will there be departments, units, divisions or functional groups in most American businesses.
   - There will be a meltdown of the barrier between leader and follower, manager and worker. Bosses, in the traditional sense, will all but disappear.

2.   Impact of technology:
   - Complex calculations can now be processed in seconds.
   - Information can be sent to multiple recipients anywhere in the world at the stroke of a computer key via electronic mail.
   - Vast amounts of information can be accessed through various search engines that can track down more data on a topic than you could ever use.
   - Google is now a verb, even though the original selection of the name for the search engine was a spelling mistake.
   - Bricks-and-mortar stores have been replaced by clicks-and-mortar online vendors who may never see a customer in person.

3.   ERP is enterprise resource planning. It is an example of an information management process that involves the interconnection of all the functional departments of an organization on one common framework. It offers the promise of improved efficiency through the deliberate elimination of waste and rework.

4.   Challenges faced with virtual management:
   - How do you manage a team that may be spread across 50 states or 20 countries?
   - The technology may be there to support conference calls or "webinars" or videoconferences, but how do you build a team when the team members never meet in person?
   - Outsourcing offers tremendous cost savings when you take advantage of lower labor costs in other countries, but how much of your proprietary information are you willing to share with this new partner in order to make the new relationship work?
   - If your company has grown on the basis of a high-quality product that you designed and manufactured in house and how do you transfer that production overseas in order to maintain that quality while working through a third-party vendor?

5.   One type exists when a group of skilled individuals form a company by communicating via computer, phone, fax or videoconference. A second type occurs when a group of companies, each of which specializes in a certain function such as manufacturing or marketing, partner together. A third type occurs when one large company outsources many of its operations by using modern technology to

transmit information to its partner companies so that it can focus on its specialty.

6. Areas covered in a code of ethics:
   - Honesty
   - Adherence to the law
   - Product safety and quality
   - Health and safety in the workplace
   - Conflicts of interest
   - Employment practices
   - Selling and marketing practices
   - Financial reporting
   - Pricing, billing, and contracting
   - Trading in securities and using confidential information
   - Acquiring and using information about competitors
   - Security
   - Payments to obtain business
   - Political activities
   - Protection of the environment

7. Questions to ask:
   - Have you defined the problem accurately?
   - How would you define the problem if you stood on the other side of the fence?
   - Whom could your decision or action injure? Can you discuss the problem with the affected parties before you make your decision?
   - Are you confident that your position will be as valid over a long period of time as it seems now?
   - Could you disclose without qualm your decision or action to your boss, your CEO, the board of directors, your family, and society as a whole?

8. The Sherman Act makes it illegal for companies to monopolize trade. The Clayton Act makes it illegal to charge different prices to different wholesale customers. The Wheeler-Lea Act bans unfair or deceptive acts or practices, including false advertising.

9. The Federal Food, Drug, and Cosmetic Act of 1938 bans the sale of impure, improperly labeled, falsely guaranteed and unhealthful foods,

drugs and cosmetics. The Consumer Product Safety Commission establishes minimum product safety standards on consumer products. Under the Truth in Lending Act of 1968, creditors are required to let consumers know how much they are paying in finance charges and interest. The Equal Credit Opportunity Act prohibits creditors from making credit decisions on the basis of discriminatory practices.

10. The three schools of thought are profit maximization, trusteeship management, and social involvement. In the 19th and early 20th centuries, business owners in the U.S. believed their role was simply to maximize the profits their companies earned. The trusteeship management philosophy recognized that owners of businesses had obligations to do more than just earn profits. During the 1960s, people began to believe that corporations should use their influence and financial resources to address social problems.

11. Social audit steps:
   - Examine social expectations, sensitivity, and past responses.
   - Examine and then set social objectives and meaningful priorities.
   - Plan and implement strategies and objectives in each program area.
   - Set budgets for resources necessary for social action and make a commitment to acquire them.
   - Monitor accomplishments or progress in each program area.

CRITICAL THINKING EXERCISES

1. Student answers will vary.

2. Student answers will vary. Technology has changed businesses from solely brick-and-mortar stores to brick-and-click stores. Inventory and shipping products have become more efficient with technology. Technology has allowed for mass customization.

3. When managing employees through observation, leaders can utilize a control model; however, by hiring work at home employees, one must use a trust method. Also, since these workers can be spread all over the world, it will be difficult to monitor employee behavior. As with any new employee, training will be required, but management must be willing to change and enable a learning culture. New forms of

communication and collaboration will be required because the employees won't be there in person.

4. In many people's opinion, this situation would be an ethical dilemma because you are deciding between essentially violating company policies and not having a nice place for you and your family to stay in L.A. Both of these are unsatisfactory options. The sense of "legal" versus "ethical" comes from company policy, which isn't very well defined.

5. a. Social responsibility includes providing a safer work environment, good benefits, a safe, high quality product line, prompt complaint handling, and honest pricing policies. The result of social audit would indicate that Mr. Furlong is running his business in a socially responsible manner, as far as he goes.

   b. Mr. Furlong's stakeholders would be his boss, the stockholders, employees, customers, competitors, suppliers and the general public.

   c. Although he would get fairly high scores from his employees in the area of social responsibility, Mr. Furlong doesn't appear to have any involvement with the community in which he operates. He could improve community relations (and even increase his customer base) by encouraging his employees to get involved in community related projects, donating time and/or money to local charities, developing a stand on local issues, improving employee-related benefits with job enrichment and employee development, and making opportunities for members of ethnic and minority groups.

PRACTICE TEST

MULTIPLE CHOICE

1. C	8. B
2. A	9. C
3. D	10. A
4. A	11. D
5. B	12. C
6. D	13. B
7. C	14. A

TRUE FALSE

1. True	8. False
2. False	9. True
3. False	10. False
4. True	11. False
5. True	12. True
6. False	13. False
7. True	14. True